T0065202

BOOKS BY JAY R. LEACH

How Should We Then Live
Behold the Man
The Blood Runs Through It
Drawn Away
Give Me Jesus
A Lamp unto My Feet
Grace that Saves
The Narrow Way
Radical Restoration in the Church
Manifestation of the True Children of God
According to Pattern
Battle Cry
Is there not a Cause?
We Would See Jesus
According to Pattern 2nd Edition
The Apostolic Rising
For His Glory
Where have all the Shepherds Gone?
Out of Babylon

OUT *of* BABYLON

"We are not Ignorant of Satan's Devices"

JAY LEACH

Trafford rev. 03/01/2023

 www.trafford.com

North America & international
toll-free: 844-688-6899 (USA & Canada)
fax: 812 355 4082

SCRIPTURE QUOTATIONS

CONTENTS

SECTION 4: LOVE AND HOLINESS

DEDICATION

To Magdalene, my beloved wife of (60 years as of January 20th, 2023), and partner on the journey of discovering this great truth. Your life looks a lot like His to me.

To the Bread of Life Ministries Int' L, our family of faith on earth, as well as those already in heaven, without whom this book might never have been written. Your hunger for truth inspires us, and your unabashed support is ever humbling to Magdalene and me. To God be the glory!

INTRODUCTION

We live in a complex time of change and conflict – accelerated by a tech/savvy society with a determined secularistic world view. For a while now, we have heard the cultural slang "digital Babylon," in this case, to bring to light the tremendous impact of technological advances especially social media on Generation Y (born 1980) & Generation Z (born 2000). With the best of intentions, we wrap our children in a world like environment of unreality catching many who leave home unprepared for the real-world environment, controlled by the unholy trinity, consisting of the world, the flesh, and the devil – through the spirit of Babylon.

They are about to enter college, job market, the military or *independence*. Unaware of the present-day cast of characters full of the spirit of Babylon standing ready to bombard them with ideologies and (false teaching). Probably, we are aware of some in our very own families. These young people after surviving their K-12 secular orientation time, begin to drift becoming disillusioned with the pluralistic society and just quietly walk away from the Bible, *the faith* of Jude 3, and fall into the religious clutches of darkness of the present age. Like an unkept garden where the tares has grown up. Our children are overcome with the mind-boggling weeds (philosophical influences) from the realm of darkness – ruled by the prince of this dark world Satan and his demonic forces.

Preachers are we supporting Satan's platform when we fail to expose him in the *minds* of our families, churches, and communities? We are at war! His footprints are everywhere in all levels of our cultures and society. Sometimes I think we tend to forget that Jesus called him the prince of this world. His pressures for "relativism" "postmodernism" "a new tolerance" and the "screen" have taken their tolls on our teens, and young adults. Most come apart when the storms of life begin to affect them, because they have no true biblical (moral) foundation as past generations.

Secularism and atheism along with paganism's comeback are becoming the norm across this nation. Why? Because people are comfortable with "nothing supernatural," as "status" "pleasure," and "entertainment," become the first priorities in the cultural lives, and homes of Americans today. Our textbooks in public education from primary through graduate level education are produced with the intention of deliberately deceiving our younger generations. They no longer have the confidence that only comes from their knowing why they believe what they believe.

Changes are coming so fast in this generation that many teenagers are simply left confused and aloft accepting (the lie), to what is right or wrong – true or false. This condition is seen in recent Barna research, which reflects that less than 34% of our teens agree that "lying is morally wrong" which creates a bigger problem. Who did they get that from? Well, our culture is also deeply confused about moral and spiritual truth, gender, and sexuality, but **the "lie"** itself says, "I don't need God!" This "lie" has been spun around and around to the point where today, no one will listen to someone else's point of view unless they *completely* agree with them.

The "screen," television, other social media, and additionally there is relativism's (claiming no absolutes), postmodernism's (deconstruction), post Covid-19's (frustrations), and many cultic beliefs that are surfacing as part of the great paradigm shift we are witnessing today. To get away from Christianity many are testing these views and many other religions, cults, philosophies, and other beliefs requiring *no Christ nor cross!* Secular humanism, critical religious theories, false prophets, and false teachers overwhelm us daily with shallow opinions, information, worldly wisdom, but little or no truth leaving our children as the test of psychology and (a therapeutic gospel) for the long-term effects on identity.

Additionally, this shift has provided a completely new definition of what it means to the lives of teenagers or young adults (allowing their feelings and herd mentality as guides). One of our goals at the Bread of life is to teach, mentor and equip Christians with a biblical worldview and shepherd leadership model using the 2 Timothy 2:2 (Jesus' multiplication model), our commission (Matthew 28:18-20), and Spiritually-developing a Christlikeness, (see Galatians 5:22, 23), throughout life.

A big difference between the biblical Christian view and the secular (no God, no Christ, no Spirit, and no saints) view is, that the secular model (simply watch the lambs); but central to the biblical world view model, we are counseled and led by the Holy Spirit to (watch *over* the lambs). The difference between the two is like day and night. Sadly, in our culture, we mostly pay attention to the negative trends, but certainly there are many positive trends also. There is much research showing the negative in constant view. But what if we would change our focus to include and support the positive also?

- What unique opportunities and challenges will parents, and Christian leaders face while attempting to pass on the faith to the next generation?
- What do parents view as most important to their identity?
- What is Gen Zers relationship to faith, parents, and other institutions?
- What do they believe about the bigger questions of life?
- How have our church cultures and society shaped them?
- How and what are they thinking about adulthood?
- Are they concerned about where their place is in life and eternity?
- Have they been introduced to the gospel, and (refreshing) Christian radio such as: the Bible Broadcasting Network (BBN), the American Family Network (AFN) and so many more?

These few questions just scratch the surface. What my wife Magdaléne and I chose to focus on to this day, made all the difference in the world. As the parents of five children, we wanted something better for them – the kind of love, peace, and joy that only comes from knowing Jesus Christ personally for the rest of their lives. We had family-town meeting (open discussion) each Tuesday night. Our Sunday mornings always began with family altar. We insisted that (all) develop holy habits of – prayer, study/ read the Bible, and other profitable books, and other Christian materials.

Our five children passed that seed on to their children and now we are seeing fruit continually being produced through the second, third and fourth generations in our own lifetime. Praise the Lord! That is what it means to watch *over*, rather than just *watch* your kids. Holy habits should be developed in every home. Of course a major contribution was my wife setting aside her career to stay at home to biblically and logistically support the children and myself (military career).

Four of our five children are ordained ministers of the gospel of Jesus Christ two along with one granddaughter are high school principals. The fifth child, manager of a AAA car care center and facility. All are Bible-believing Christ followers. I have noticed since the COVID shut down quite a number of families have made the choice of mothers and in some cases fathers setting aside their career or working at home to support and raise their children together. Praise God! I realize this way of life is foreign to the minds of many today!

One of God's promises for those who are His: "And my God shall supply all your need according to His riches in glory by Christ Jesus." (Philippians 4:19 NKJV) Don't let the spirit of Babylon (this world) fool you! Acquiring more stuff is temporary – but our children are eternal!

If we convert sinners, but the world converts – our Millennials, Gen Zers, and our other young people, we are right back where we started.

Some readers will pick this book and think it is only about outer evangelism toward Gen Zers. But we need to widen our scope to include inward evangelism, which includes our homes and church family which reaches not only Gen Zers, but all of our children, our youth, our young adults (both married and single). The early church had to first reach inside Jerusalem, to their families, friends, and neighbors, before reaching outside to Judea, Samaria, and to the ends of the earth (see Acts 1:8).

God did not send His Son to take vengeance on hungry, thirsty sinners. Jesus came to save sinners! That was the whole reason He went to the cross:

"For God did not send His Son into the world to condemn the world, but that the world through Him might be saved." (John 3:17 NKJV)

At His first coming, Jesus came so that **the world through Him might be saved. When Jesus comes again, He will come in judgment upon those who refused His offer of regeneration. To believe in Jesus Christ is to receive life (vv. 15 and 16) and avoid judgment. A person who does not believe, not only misses life but is condemned already.**

People offer many excuses for not accepting Christ. Some put it on the presence of hypocrites in the church. Others cite the inability to believe some of the truths about Christ or the gospel – thus, leaving themselves open for the *"Big Lie."* These are merely attempts to conceal a heart in rebellion against God.

The ultimate reason people do not come
to Christ is they don't want to.

One who does come to the "light" not only believes, but he or she also *identifies* with the light so that their works can be seen as things done with unity in Christ. Our task for ourselves and our children is to come into the knowledge of the truth. That is, "Trust in the LORD with all your heart, and do not lean on your own understanding. In all your ways acknowledge Him and He will make straight your paths." (Proverbs 3:5, 6 ESV)

Remember, no matter what you (believers) are going through, Christ is the ultimate answer. The Word of God promises "*for those who love God all things work together for good....*" (Romans 8:28 ESV). Have faith in God! Get out of the flesh, stop trying to fix the impossible – the battle is not yours, it's the Lord's. Again, the Gospel of Jesus Christ saves in every group and every Era including Generations Y and Gen Zers. "Salvation belongs to the LORD." (Psalms 3:8 NKJV) The watchword for the child of God today is, "No weapon formed against you shall prosper."(Isaiah 54:17 NKJV)

Jay Leach, pastor, teacher, apologist
In His Service, Fayetteville, NC

Section One

SHIFTING CHURCH CULTURE

Chapter One

THE DIVINE STRATEGY

*"I therefore, the prisoner of the Lord, beseech you to walk
worthy of the calling with which you were called, with all
lowliness and gentleness, with longsuffering, bearing with
one another in love, endeavoring to keep the unity of the
Spirit in the bond of peace."* (Ephesians 4:1-3 NKJV)

A man had a fondness for asking, "If you were to receive a million dollars tomorrow, what would you do with it?" It was his way of finding out what came first in a person's desires. What does come first? It is a leading question. Though a person must think the basics of food and clothing, he should not think of them first. Thus, Jesus sums up the teaching of Matthew 6:19-34. What is center for us? Our Christian life should be like a solar system. Christ the sun, is our personal focus of the kingdom, and all else revolving around Him. Could our sin be that we are not "bad," but that we live for the "good" instead of the "best."

"But seek ye first the kingdom of God and His righteousness; and all these things shall be added unto you." (Matthew 6:33 KJV) The word "shall" is a command; which indicates that God will take care of the other things. Christ goes on to tell us several reasons why living for material things is foolish. For one thing material things do not last. Exquisite fabrics were treasured by the Jews, yet moths continuously ruined them. Rust ruins metal; and thieves steal riches. However, treasures used for the glory of God are deposited in heaven where they last throughout eternity. The way people use wealth provides a good indication of the condition of their hearts.

If we spend our time and money only on more and more stuff (materialism) and neglect God, then our hearts are on material things and not fixed on God. We find a good example of this when we compare Abraham and Lot in (see Genesis 13:5-18). If the church strategy we are employing is not aligned with God's divine strategy, why teach and train new generations to continue more of the same?

GOD'S DIVINE CONCEPT

Many people to include some clergy think that the incarnation of Christ came at His birth and ended when Jesus ascended into the clouds. The word "incarnate" means "to take bodily form." When God in eternity past chose to demonstrate to humanity His love and the new life He offered us, His concept included Him incarnating Himself, by taking on our form, and living among us, while sharing our human experience. God became flesh and dwelt among us. Jesus was the incarnation of God, God in human flesh – the God-man. In spite of the belief of some, the incarnation did not end with the earthly life of Christ. Today, Christ's body does His work around the world. It is a corporate body, made up of millions of people like you and me, the world over, from all nations – the body of Christ, called the Church!

In the Book of Acts, Luke presents a sequel to his previous account, the Gospel of Christ's work among humanity according to Luke. Yet Jesus, Himself only appears in the first eleven verses of the Book of Acts. Please note in Acts 1:11, Jesus ascends into heaven. Yet the record of His work on earth continues for twenty-eight more chapters. How? The rest of Acts is a record of His *new body the church!*

When His body lives and moves in and by the Spirit, it is then the physical extension of the life of Jesus to the whole world. Jesus' physical life began at the moment the virgin Mary conceived of the Holy Spirit, Jesus' divine conception, (see prayerfully Luke 1:26-38) and has continued uninterrupted right up to this 'present moment, around two thousand years. That is God's glorious and all-important concept. What happened among that small gathering in Judea and Galilee two thousand years ago continues to this day, but on a worldwide scale, permeating societies everywhere and every aspect of human life.

Once people discover this *truth* for their own lives, they are transformed. Their relationship with God is exciting and they become powerfully useful for God. This is the Christian life. God's intention is that we all grow up into mature men and women transformed by the indwelling presence of the Holy Spirit. Discipleship, then, is working *these truths* into our practical, everyday lives. The Book of Acts is more than a history of the church's beginning – it is an "operations manual" for the Body of Christ. Through the first eight verses in the first chapter of Acts, God made clear His divine strategy:

"But ye <u>shall receive power</u>, after that the Holy Ghost is come upon you; and ye <u>shall</u> be witnesses unto Me both in Jerusalem, and in all Judea, and in Samaria, and unto the uttermost part of the earth." (**Acts 1:8 KJV**) Emphasis added.

It is so refreshing to rediscover the (Divine) strategy which God has designed for every member of His (entire) body of Christ to *influence* the world. That is, His power (the indwelling Holy Spirit) who raised Jesus Christ from the grave. The same Spirit is in us also (we, the body of Christ is God's counter-culture) to the spirit of Babylon (the world). He gives the true believers power individually and corporately to receive: His teaching (revealed truth) of God's Word, His leading, and His guidance in all things. All done through Christ's mandate that we "love one to another." (see John 15:12) In that same chapter, Christ moves from the love of the brethren to the hatred of the world. Why does the world[1] hate Christians?

---

[1]   Accessed 5/20/22 Bing: "The world" means the whole system of society that is opposed to Christ and God, the Father. It is made up of people and organizations, philosophies and purposes that are anti-Christian. "The world" has a prince, Satan (see John 14:30).

- Because it first hated Christ – and we belong to Him (1 John 3:13).
- Because we no longer belong to the world (I John 4:5 and John 17:14).
- Because the world has rejected His Word (v. 20).
- Because the world does not know the Father (see 16:1-3).
- Because the world's sin has been exposed by Christ.

Any church that *fails or refuses* to see this amazing concept will substitute flesh induced in-house busy work, programs, church traditions, and pressure politics as a means to influence society.

THE CHURCH DOWN THROUGH THE YEARS

In 2 Timothy 3, through the power of the indwelling Holy Spirit, Paul looks down through the centuries and with his prophetic eyes tells <u>us what to expect in the last days.</u> He gives his charge in the light of the future of the church. "The last days" is a period that began with the life and ministry of Christ on earth (see Hebrews 1:1-2). However, the New Testament indicates that "the last days" refers particularly to "the state of the church" before the coming of Christ. These shall be "perilous" times, that is "difficult, hard to deal with." This is the same word used in Matthew 8:28 to describe the Gadarene demoniac. Because people will "depart from the faith" they will believe the "doctrines of devils" (see 2 Timothy 4:1), this world will become a "demoniac graveyard" just as in Gadara. We are in these last days; which are marked by "self-love." The media certainly insures that we all know it by exploiting these characteristics in verses 5-8:

- This self-love will lead to a grasping attitude and boastful spirit.
- True affection will almost disappear – while unnatural affection will prevail.
- We live in a "heady" and "reckless" world as fierce and savage conduct increases.

- There will be much religion in the last days – but it will be a mere imitation, of godliness without the life-changing power of God.
- The departing of the faith that Paul predicted in (2 Thessalonians 2) is here, but there is still plenty of religion.
- The Bible continues to be a national best seller, yet the crime rate increases and problems multiply.
- True Christians are in the minority.
- These false teachers of Paul's day preyed especially upon women who were loaded with sins and led astray by their lusts, women who were "ever learning" but who never really came to an understanding of the truth.

Paul compared the apostate teachers to the Egyptian magicians Jannes and Jambres, who opposed Moses by *imitating what he did* (see Exodus 7:11). Satan is an imitator, and his imitation gospel, and imitation church <u>will spread in the last days.</u> Every local church should get into the Word of God; since these satanic imitators are going to continue. What should the church do? Continue to be faithful to Christ and His Word. If every pastor, Bible teacher, and Sunday School teacher would be faithful to teach every Christian to understand, defend, the true Word of God, and proclaim their beliefs in an age of increasing moral and spiritual relativism – Satan's disciples would be defeated!

NOTE TIMOTHY'S RELATIONSHIP WITH THE BIBLE

Since these satanic seducers are going to continue, what should Christians do? In verses 14-17, Timothy's life is profiled. It began when he was a child and learned the Old Testament Scriptures from his *mother* and *grandmother*. They did not simply teach the facts of the Bible; but they gave him assurance and understanding:

- Timothy *knew for himself* the truth of God's Word.
- He did not depend on others to defend the Word of God – for him.

5

- This Word imparted faith to him (see Romans 10:17), and this faith in Christ brought salvation.

What is the purpose of the Bible?

1. Salvation
2. Christian living – the Word of God is profitable for teaching (doctrine), (reproof), setting things right.
3. Correction, and discipline (instruction).
4. It enables the child of God to become a man or woman of God, matured in the things of the Lord.

The great need among churches and Christians today is to return to the Bible. Every pastor and teacher must be an apologist[2] (defender of the Christian faith). If the churches do not get back to God's Word – the satanic deceivers will take over with their religious lies. Four functions of apologetics distinguished by great Christian apologists throughout church history:

1. The first function – is *vindication or proof* – it involves gathering evidence for the Christian faith. The goal being to develop a positive case for Christianity as a belief system that should be accepted. Drawing out implications of the biblical worldview so they can be seen and contrasted with other worldviews.
2. The second function – is *defense* – in involves clarifying the Christian position in light of misunderstandings and misinterpretations; answering objections, criticisms, or questions from non-Christians; and in general clearing away any intellectual difficulties that nonbelievers claim stand in the way of their coming to faith.
3. The third function – is *refutation* – of opposing beliefs. This function focuses on answering the arguments non-Christians give in support of their own beliefs. Most

---

[2] The word *apologia* appears 17 times in the noun or verb form in the New Testament and translated "defense" or "vindication" in every case. The idea of offering a defense of the faith is evident in Philippians 17:16 and especially in 1 Peter 3:15.

apologists agree that refutation cannot stand alone, since proving non-Christian religion or philosophy to be false does not prove that Christianity is true.

4. The fourth function – is *persuasion* – by this we do not mean merely convincing people that Christianity is true but persuading them to apply its truth to their life. This function focuses on bringing non-Christians to the point of commitment. The apologist's motive is not merely to win an intellectual argument, but to persuade people to commit their lives and eternal future into the hands of Jesus Christ, our Savior.[3]

GATHER DIFFERENTLY AND BETTER

With theological and biblical precision, people pointed out that the people insisted we stop saying, "go to church." They were adamant that people *are* the church; they don't *go* to the church. The church is not a building, and the building is not the church. But the church facility is the place where the church gathers. The church facility may be a traditional church building. It may be a house. It may be a grove of trees. Still, it is a place where the church gathers.

The writer of the Book of Hebrews wants the members of the church to encourage and·motivate one another to acts of love and good works. He is adamant in this desire and hope: let us, *"not forsake the assembling of ourselves together, as is the manner of some, but exhorting one another, and so much the more as you see the Day approaching."* (Hebrews 10:25 NKJV) Is that clear? As fellow believers, we encourage one another when we meet together. The gathered church is important. During the pandemic we missed the in person, gathered church tremendously.

The quarantine, however, also gave us an opportunity to reflect. As church leaders planned for reentry of the gathered church – they began asking some important questions: Are we using our church facilities to maximum stewardship? What can we do differently?

---

[3] CSB Apologetics Study Bible, Article *"What is Apologetics?* (Holman Bible Publishers Nashville, TN 2017) XXV

What can we do better? Many have decided to do things differently. I hope and pray that we all be excited and encouraged. Remember, Jesus said, "Fear not!" Don't let the unknown be a source of fear. This is not a time for business as usual. Remember, the pandemic did not catch God by surprise. He is working His own plan or program for His Church.

SIMPLE CHURCH

I'm sure you will agree when I say, the pandemic was a wake-up call for the church like none other. This is a time to hear what the Spirit is saying to the churches. Be prepared to make necessary positive changes to move our churches forward. Now that we are "out of Babylon" – it is now time for us (the body of Christ) to enter this new land of possibilities with hope, promise, and enthusiasm.

One key to being a simple church – is to focus on those areas that are primarily essential to the church's mission – and, if possible, eliminate all things that are nonessential.

Many of our churches had busied themselves trying to do too many things that were not essential to the core mission of the congregation. Prior to the pandemic many gauged the health of a congregation by the number of times people came to the facility for worship services, rehearsals, auxiliary meetings, programs, and events. A busy building *was* a sign of life and health.

The full church calendar

Sadly, many local churches have simply attempted to return to business as usual; which means a return to the full church calendar (of scheduled events). Oftentimes prior to COVID-19 people were so busy "going to church" that they failed to evangelize and do missions in their community – the Great Commission is a command of our King and Savior, Jesus Christ to the body of Christ, the church, and please know, that this *a command*, not a mere suggestion or recommendation! Prayerfully and carefully study (Acts 1:8; John 14; Matthew 28:16-20; 2 Timothy 2:2).

STUDY GUIDE: WORKSHEET AND REFLECTION
CHAPTER 1

1. In Matthew 6, Christ goes on to tell us several reasons why living for material things is foolish. List 3 of His reasons in the space below.

2. Can our sin be that we are not bad, but we live for the _____ instead of the _____.

3. "Incarnate" means to _____
    _____ _____.

4. God's intention is that we all grow up to maturity transformed by the indwelling _____ _____.

5. The Book of Acts is an Operations Manual for the _____ ___ _____.

6. How does Acts 1:8 fit int God's divine strategy?

7. List the four functions of Apologetics below:
    1.
    2.
    3.
    4.

Chapter Two

DEFINING CHURCH CULTURE

"For God is not a God of confusion but of peace." (1 Corinthians 14:33 ESV)

W_e are told in Romans 5:5, *"Now hope does not disappoint, because the love of God has been poured out in our hearts by the Holy Spirit who was given to us." NKJV.* The hope that Christians have of their future glory with God will not disappoint them by being unfulfilled. They will not be put to shame or humiliated because of their hope!

The New Covenant gives the believer full confidence in the love of God which has been poured out on him or her and the Holy Spirit is given to them (see Romans 5:5; 8:9). The Holy Spirit dwells in believers and constantly encourages them in their hope in God.

UNHEALTHY SAINTS

The work of the ministry cannot be effectively carried out in a weak and unhealthy church. At the beginning of the COVID-19 epidemic many of our local churches were on life support. The indications are that many have already succumbed due to pre-existing spiritual diseases. Therefore, it is no surprise that the Holy Spirit's pattern for the proper functioning of Christ's body includes a plan for keeping the believers in shape and healthy.

Christ, Himself *"gave some to be apostles, some prophets, some evangelists, and some pastors and teachers, for the equipping of the saints for the work of ministry, for the edifying of the body of Christ, till we all come to the unity of the faith and of the knowledge of the Son of God, to a perfect man, to the measure of the stature of the fullness of Christ."* (Ephesians 4:11-13 NKJV)

Sadly, even though the Book of Acts has already given a model to follow – many churches turn to the business world for a pattern. That said, the church should not be afraid to learn from healthy organizations and (be eclectic) adapt the right practices. And even though the word *"culture"* is not found in the Bible, its concept is found throughout its pages.

Research shows 90% of Americans believe
America has a mental crisis.

By the Holy Spirit's leading, the early church shifted their culture several times to their changing world. The apostles were a lot more adoptive and flexible than we could ever imagine – and the church thrived in a *fluid environment not* bound by the boundaries we have come to accept today. One thing for sure, the adjustments made for survival of the COVID-19 pandemic have removed many traditional barriers to technological change in long-standing institutions. When the order to quarantine was handed down there was no time to object to digital innovation.

** My purpose in writing this book is to help local churches to realize their need for reshaping church culture to reach and retain a new generation, we need to *first* get a handle and clarification on what we mean by "church culture.

CULTURE AND VISION

Some years ago, I submitted a resume to a church's search committee, that was seeking a pastor. As we navigated through the interview, one of the officers asked about my vision for the church. Somehow in the discussion two other words were being used interchangeably with vision: culture, and mission. Actually, it became apparent that we had different working definitions for the word "culture."

Culture is an umbrella term which encompasses the *social behavior,* and *norms* found in human societies, as well as the knowledge, beliefs, arts, laws, customs, capabilities, and habits in these racial, religious, or social groups.[4] In most cases, your church already has some form of mission and vision statements. Many times they are repeated from the pulpit or posted on a banner, and sometimes mounted in lovely picture frames and strategically placed somewhere in vestibules or the lobby, and definitely in all of the churches' literature and publications.

While most churches talk about the mission, sadly, there are many churches that never give even a favorable mention of them. Now, in my experience, church culture is often accepted as an *unchanging reality.* In many churches, unchanging means, "we have never done it like that." Often called, "the seven last words of a dying church."

Because something has been practiced in a church for the past century, does not necessarily mean it's right. Likewise, because a thing has not been practiced for a century in the church does not mean it's wrong.

Your mission and vision reflect what your church believes – the what and the why of what you do. Your church's "culture" reflects how your church behaves – how you do what you do as standard operating procedures. Planned or unplanned, every church has its own unique culture; which is often overlooked. Our success in

---

[4]   Accessed 2/15/22, heeps://www.thoughtco.com/culture-definition -- 4135409

revivals and our ability to cast a powerful vision are dependent upon a healthy church culture to carry it.

An unhealthy church culture will annihilate your vision. Until we understand our church's culture, our vision will be blurred, and our churches will *decline*! What we are failing to see in many local churches is how church culture – not vision – is the most dynamic key in revival. Remember! You *can* cast a vision – but you *cannot* cast a culture. Vision flows from top down. Culture spews *out* from the bottom up.

Until we understand our organizational (in the house) culture, our vision will remain blurred, and our church will continue to decline. My point here is a clear vision is mandatory for success in the church! The Bible says, *"Where there is no vision, the people perish."* (Proverb 29:18 KJV)

THE POWER OF CULTURE

Church culture can be helpful to the congregation, or it can be harmful. Harmful for most because many churches deny its existence. It can be used to build strong families, churches, and communities. In spite our beautifully composed vision and mission statements presenting the proper model – the church culture paints the true picture of where we really are with them!

The church culture is defined by how the church is run and get along. That is, how the *personalities* within interact with each other, and how the infrastructure of the church is set up. Again, while we are fine tuning our vision, we must remember it is our culture that determines the health of our churches, particularly, how effectively it is in reaching a new generation.

The church culture we create can attract or repel God's favor. While there may be moral corruption in the church, a church doesn't have to stoop so low to have an unhealthy culture.

For example, an unhealthy church culture could be the result of:

- Spiritual hearing
- Spiritual blindness
- Dead works

- Dead traditions
- Disorganization
- Poor decision-making
- Politics
- Carnality
- Denial of the Holy Spirit, His gifts and ministries
- Unbelief
- Unspiritual
- Pride
- Political correctness
- Cliques and family feuds
- Increasing ethnic and racial bias
- Favoritism
- Attitude toward the unsaved
- Attitude toward visitors

The above list is only a sample of many other possible issues to be considered, *"For God is not the author of confusion but of peace, as in all the churches of the saints."* (1 Corinthians 14:33 NKJV) It seems that each denomination has selected and promoted a word, a verse or passage of Scripture or philosophy (i.e., "birds of a feather flock together" "individual autonomy") as the identifier of their basic cultural beliefs, and values (mostly unspoken). Ask about the New Covenant in most local churches – it is unheard of even among some of the hierarchy.

After more than 500 years we have yet to reach a consensus bodily on the Holy Spirit, His purpose, His gifts, and His ministries *for all* of the body of Christ. And that, in spite of the many direct biblical commands and directives made by Jesus Christ, and the apostles. It is written!

CURE FOR UNHEALTHY CHURCH CULTURE

Many believers are distraught over what they see going on in the local churches of this nation, today. Ezekiel experienced similar conditions in Israel in his day. God's people were in disarray and the priests were obsessed with their own affairs and welfare, as they piled up riches for themselves. They cheated the people and lived off the offerings while the people suffered.

People wandered about everywhere looking for *spiritual food –* *with no shepherds to feed them, lead them, and bind up their wounds.* At the same time, the Scripture says, the Israelites were still living in sin and trusting in their own righteousness. God told Ezekiel,

> *"And they come to you as people come, and they sit before you as* *my people, and they hear what you say but they will not do it, for with* *lustful talk in their mouths they act; their heart is set on their gain.* *And behold, you are to them like one who sings lustful songs with a* *beautiful voice plays well on an instrument, **for they hear what you*** ***say, but they will not do it.*** *"* (Ezekiel 33:31-32 ESV) Emphasis added throughout.

Here we contrast the actions and attitudes of the exiles with the life of God's prophet Ezekiel. The exiles had claimed to go to the prophet to receive God's revelation, but their actions and behavior were not in compliance with their stated beliefs and values. Their true desire was for entertainment – but not for divine enlightenment. If the fall of Jerusalem failed to spiritually awaken them, nothing would. Yet it would open their eyes to the divine truth of Ezekiel's preaching.

For years we've been convincing ourselves that a perfect vision and strategy does the work, but those components <u>do not force us</u> <u>to change the prevailing attitudes and behavioral patterns of the</u> <u>church.</u> It does not address the volumes of spoken and unspoken messages that *sway* our church in a particular direction – no matter what vision or strategy we might cast. Until we thoroughly understand our church's culture:

- behavior toward leadership,
- how we do things,
- how we act toward strangers

our vision will be buried, and our church will continue to decline.

You are probably seeing by now that church culture often flies under the radar. It is often evasive, unexplained, unnoticed, or just ignored but it determines how your church responds to your leadership. To change it requires less talking and more listening. What kind of church culture are you creating? That is an important question, especially to the post-COVID-19 church. Your answer to the question will either carry you or bury you!

Prior to 2000, church culture was relatively solid and predictable, built by (the Great Generation) which included returning military and civilian personnel, from WWI and WWII (1925-1945) to communities across America – and the Baby Boomers generation (born 1946-1964). Certainly, visioning was prevalent for leaders in that type of culture. During that period churches carried a basic Judeo-Christian worldview and could work on a clear vision that sharpened their identity, focused their callings, organized their infrastructure, and departments, producing a list of ideas about God, morality, sexuality, family, marriage, motherhood, spirituality, and religion were understood from a Christian perspective. People who broke the rules (were called into question), but everyone was assuming pretty much the same rules.

During this period, the church became
department and program driven.

Most present-day pastors were trained under that paradigm and most of their ministerial trainees continue to run their churches that way (programs) no matter what *changes* they implement – *and therein lies the problem.* As one writer puts it: "Too many church leaders are perfectly equipped to reach a world that no longer exists."

I have watched this "cataclysmic transformation" from the 1960's and 80's to the present. I've thought through, privileged to lecture on it on three continents of the world, and written many manuscripts, and published 18 books about it – I hope and pray that by God's grace, this look-back will allow me some success in analyzing what is happening today and what Christians can do about it. Certainly, we are not about retaining or recovering a long-gone 20thcentury culture, but we must:

1. <u>Preach and teach the true gospel of Jesus Christ clearly in our own time!</u>
2. <u>Bless the culture and the world with God-honoring holy and righteous living!</u>

The changed culture in which we presently live is the only one our young readers have known. Atmosphere is important to young and old alike. It's about creating an environment conducive to love, relationship, and growth – particularly among young people.

Some Millennials will voice that they are <u>not</u> leaving our churches because of our vision, or lack of vision, <u>but because of our culture.</u> They are leaving <u>because of the way the members act and the way they do things.</u> They are not leaving because of the truths we believe. If your church is legalistic, they will leave you.

Sadly, the average Black millennial in this country, no longer defines a vital spiritual life as knowledge of and communication with the infinite-yet personal Creator and Lord of heaven and earth who is revealed in the Bible.

If your church tradition and culture remains the 80's – 90's model you will lose GEN Zers, because you have already lost their de-churched parents (Millennials).

De-churched Christians are those who love Jesus, but for one reason or another have left their local churches. While we should desire to understand our culture *in order to bear witness to Jesus in it* – we must avoid compromising to its *expectations* just to get its affirmation! We must be mindful, as the church, we must call all cultures along with ourselves in every generation to the rule that judges all other rules – the rule of faith, the Word of God.

"Too many church leaders are perfectly equipped to reach a world that no longer exists."

Emerging generations (Y and Z) are more likely to attend a Bible study and to participate in outside ministry opportunities for both instructional and practical learning and fellowship alongside people who are *like* them. Many of our Black Y and Z generations want nothing to do with Christ nor the church, basically due to a lack of knowledge. The Black Church is being shunned by many of our young people; since our culture has deemed it to be antiquated, narrow, and uncompromising!

While much of the church is holding to the faith and the Word of God. Sadly, our churches have received such a bad critique from us. Many of the Y and Z generations are growing up never having seen the inside of a church building. I sense this generation is desperately seeking *emotional refuge* and *peer engagement*. Notice:

1. In 2001 they were shocked by the scene of planes flying into the twin towers (9/11).
2. They have coped with a COVID pandemic, which served as a wakeup call, revealing our unpreparedness for such a world-reaching crisis.
3. They have wrestled with unaccountable justice systems.
4. They have struggled with systemic racism, white supremacy, privilege, and so-called place in systems and society.
5. They have witnessed a disastrous, and unpeaceful government transition (2020).
6. For many young people it presented their first opportunity to vote or participate in campaign work.
7. They are forced to have to deal with gun violence, home invasions, systemic racism and in redlining public and private housing, and growing poverty.

The bottom line is, reaching, teaching, and retaining (discipling) *a new generation* depends on what kind of church culture we are creating. We begin by analyzing our church culture – and though it is not an easy task in fact, it is an impossible task in the flesh. Many of us look but are overrode by the familiar. Church means change! Note the changes made in the early churches in the Book of Acts and the Epistles. The Scripture *says,*

"For the mind that is set on the flesh is hostile to God, for it does not submit to God's law; indeed, it cannot. *Those who are in the flesh cannot please God* You, however, are not in the flesh, but in the Spirit, if in fact the Spirit dwells in you (see Romans 5:5). *Anyone who does not have the Spirit of Christ does not belong to Him*" (see Romans 8:7-8 ESV, also see Ezek. 36:25-27; 37:1-30, Hebrews 8-10). Emphasis added.

In fact, an especially impossible task for all who attempt it "in the flesh," but "not so" in the power of the Holy Spirit (within us) as Christ commanded. The Spirit gave us the Gospel of Christ, His indwelling Presence and His Spiritual gifts for the proper operations in the Body of Christ, the church. "Not by might nor by power, but by My Spirit says the LORD of hosts." (Zechariah 4:6 NKJV)

A worldly-minded leader does more harm to the church none of the above works for them. God works by His Spirit – not ours! That not only goes for the church, but the home and society as well. Israel left Babylon and arrived home to rebuild the Temple (God's will) but decided to scrap His idea and build tall-ceiled houses for themselves (see the Book of Ezra).

DO NOT LOVE THE WORLD

Some pastors and other church leaders knew that the example of our work is as it was with the Israelites in rebuilding temple. Once *They were "Out of Babylon"* progress was hindered (by the men since the 1960's) in the rebuilding by the Spirit of God.

Many of our young Black Millennials and Gen Zers are treated like weeds in many of our churches as well as homes, not wanted, ignored and destroyed by us (selfish parents). In short, they have doubts about twenty-first-century churches who doubt the validity and call of women who work as leaders in every other space but the church. Much of this tension, as with issues of sexuality, are rooted in scriptural interpretations that have shaped church doctrine and church tradition over biblical revelation. In many cases, congregations who are viewed by millennials and Gen Zers as oppressive or "outdated" in this area are simply living by the Word of God in a godless society. Now having said that, following the

Word of God as our rule of authority causes us (the body of Christ) to follow its precepts and direction (lead of the Spirit of course). Since slavery our fore parents relied on the Lord's help, and He delivered! Today it hurts my heart to see so many of our people willing to just give up and be ruled by and influenced by in this case, church culture.

Knowing that, moving by *any* spirit other than the Holy Spirit is emphatically "of the flesh" and (cannot progress) because the spirit of Babylon (covers the natural world) being of the devil, who Jesus said is the prince of this world, will *naturally* enslave you. The apostle Peter admonishes us,

I am warning you ahead of time, dear friends. Be on guard so that you will not be carried away by the errors of these wicked people and lose your own secure footing. Rather, you must grow in the grace and knowledge of our Lord and Savior Jesus Christ. All glory to him, both now and forever! Amen. (2 Peter 3:17-18 NLT)

The apostle John admonishes,

"Do not love the world or the things in the world. If anyone loves the world, the love of the Father is not in Him. For all that is in the world – the lust of the flesh, the lust of the eyes, and the pride of life – is not of the Father but is of the world. And the world is passing away, and the lust of it; but he who does the will of God abides forever." (1 John 2:15-17 NKJV)

The world (Babylon) is characterized by these three lusts, John was probably alluding to different ways believers could be lured away from loving and worshipping God:

- The lust of the flesh refers to desires for sinful pleasure.
- The lust of the eyes refers to covetousness or materialism (stuff).
- The pride of life refers to being proud about one's possessions and/or position in the world (consumerism, status).

In verse 17 John highlights the shortness of life. He warns: To be *consumed* with this life is to be *unprepared* for the next. What a tragedy to invest our life and resources in what will not last!

DECEPTIONS OF THE LAST HOUR

"Little children, it is the last hour; and as you have heard that the Antichrist[5] is coming, even now many antichrists have come, by which we know that it is the last hour. They went out from us, but they were not of us, for if they had been of us, they would have continued with us; but they went out that they might be manifest, that none of them were of us." (1 John 2:18-19 NKJV)

John saw the rise of those who deny the truth of Christ from within the body of Christ (the church) as an indication of the beginning of the end of all things. Unless we repent and seek the Spirit's guidance in everything – we fail!" Notice, especially (the Spirit's role) in the chapters that follow. As the church moves forward into future decades, we are challenged to continue read and study widely especially the biblical text itself – to reshape our understanding of God and gender roles in the church and society and seek to embrace love for all.

PATRIARCHY IN THE BLACK CHURCH

In the Black church, patriarchy has really impacted everything from the leadership of the Black church to the working definition of what it means to be a "good Christian man" or a "good Christian woman." Walk into any number of Black churches on Sunday, and the face of the leadership is predominately male. The patriarchy has just made it very hard for women, millennials, and Gen Zers to really flourish.

---

[5]   Note: Antichrists is a combination of two Greek words: *anti,* meaning "instead of" or "against," and *christos,* meaning "anointed one." Antichrists means those who seek to take the place of Christ. The many antichrists are the false teachers John opposed in this letter.

I was approached and asked if Blacks who were raised in Christian homes are abandoning Christianity for African faiths? The frustrations of young people who had begun to doubt some of the teachings of the Christian tradition (but mainly church tradition) and the trustworthiness of Christian leaders and were seeking spiritualty that is more Afrocentric. These groups are really thinking through what it means to make it together, and really thinking through models of leadership that are non-hierarchical – that make space for people who have traditionally been on the margins to come into the center, and really a kind of embodying collective leadership.

Recently, I had a conversation with a young man who had joined such a religion. Since he was coming from a denominational church, my question to him was, "What are you going to do with Jesus?" He told me he was going to hang on to Christ. I have read over time about that smorgasbord of religion, a little of this and that. As I stated in an earlier section. This is an apostate, one who has heard the gospel even professed to be a follower of Christ. But at some point, they turn their backs on Jesus Christ, the Savior. Actually, they are non-Christians. Their commitment wasn't authentic, and neither was their decision.

In his book *Black Millennials & the Church*, Joshua L. Mitchell's Research suggests that black Millennials desire spiritual experiences and teaching where their blackness is reflected, and it is no surprise that African religious traditions are increasing in popularity among this generation.[6] As this generation seeks to find their identities, many are researching their ancestry and exploring the customs, languages, and spiritualities, associated with their countries of origin.

SHIFTING AWAY FROM CHRIST

One lady expressed; I did grow up in the church. It was me doing a journey of self-discovery that changed my religious beliefs.

---

[6] Joshua L. Mitchell, *Black Millennials and the Church, Meet Me Where I Am,* (Judson Press, Valley Forge, PA 2018) 98.

And so I believe it was when I was reading Ephesians 6:5 that says, "Slaves, obey thy earthly master as you would me your God," and I was like "that can't be right." And so that got me searching for what I found to be fallacies or inconsistencies in the Bible. She stated that she found so many of them – I couldn't believe it. Thus she turned to Kemetic spirituality.[7] I was finding that a lot of [the Bible] was, what I thought at the time, just copying of the original stories of the gods and goddesses. Ra, Horus, Set, and all of those Egyptian gods and goddesses. After downloading a book on my tablet, I couldn't stop reading and needless to say the TV took over as the babysitter, then sleepless nights began with periods without eating. It was like, "I can't stop learning." I couldn't put the book down and after two weeks I found there was a sense of awakening after, I was changed. I asked to be divinely guided to do this. "I see the world differently." That's when I started to find different things and new interests such as herbs and stuff. Like Shamanism,[8] I came across articles about it; which she tries then one day I was divinely guided toward Tarot cards. I'll go and find a few readers, and then the next day I'm divinely guided to do this, and I'm divinely guided to do that. So right now I call myself an Omnist, which means that I take different parts of different spiritualities, and different religions and I create a spirituality that is custom to myself.

My friend said, "So you are just taking the good parts of all religions and using those?" And I said, "That's exactly what I'm doing." Is that so wrong to do? Because, while I do feel like the Bible is still riddled with fallacies and inconsistencies, I think there's some beautiful messages that I take from the Bible. There are still ways that I use the Bible even with my numerology and things. But I do not believe in the traditional sense, anymore, of heaven and hell. And I believe you create your own heaven, and as Omnist, this is how I look at life: I think that all paths lead to God. My theory, she continues, is that you can see things in three ways: scientifically, religiously, or spiritually. But it's all the same thing. For instance, if you are a religious person, a Christian, you are going to talk about Adam and Eve. If you are a scientific person, you are going to talk

---

[7]   Ibid. 99-104

[8]   Ibid.

about atoms and electrons, and if you are a spiritual person, you might go to Egyptian spirituality and talk about Asar and Aset. Simply from reading this, you should know that there's a struggle involved in this transition. There are many such discoveries in this country and the rest of West. The apostle Paul says,/

"Now the Spirit expressly says that in latter times some will depart from the faith, giving heed to deceiving spirits and doctrines of demons ...." (1 Timothy 4:1 NKJV)

Throughout Paul's letters, the Spirit speaks warning already about the coming of false doctrines and that the church would see apostasy, a falling away from the faith (see 2 Thessalonians 2). That warning continues to hold true today in our churches. Paul points out the cause as the satanic influence of demons so that professed believers deny the basic doctrines of the Bible. The problem here is not with the head, but with the heart! These false teachers are marked for example:

- They read the Word but explain it away through their self-serving lies.
- They preach one thing but practice another.
- They are hypocrites.
- They teach a false piety namely, asceticism, that is abstaining from marriage and certain foods.

Just as "healthy" doctrine promotes spiritual health, so the foolish myths of false teachers will produce spiritual sickness. Spiritual food and spiritual exercise are a happy combination! It is suggested here that Timothy was leaning toward asceticism, the discipling of the body; and that Paul is here teaching him to emphasize spiritual disciplines and exercises more than physical. If some Christians would put as much energy and enthusiasm into spiritual things as they do athletics and body-building, how much stronger they and their churches would be! Paul admits, "Bodily exercise profits for al little while." "But spiritual exercise, practicing the Word of God is profitable for this life and the life to come." (see 1 Timothy 4:8; Hebrews 4:14)

STUDY GUIDE: WORKSHEET AND REFLECTIONS
CHAPTER 2

1. The New Covenant gives the believer full confidence in the love of God which has been poured out on them and the Holy Spirit is given to them (see Romans 5:5; 8:9).

2. The Holy Spirit's pattern for the proper functioning of the body of Christ keeps the believer in _____ and _____.

3. Even though the word _____ is not found in the Bible, it's _____ is found throughout its pages.

4. _____ is an umbrella term which encompasses the social behaviors, and norms found in human societies.

5. Your church's culture reflects how the church _____.

6. De-churched Christians are those who love Jesus but for one _____ or another they have _____ their _____ _____.

7. Why are Generations Y and Z leaving the churches?

Chapter Three

HOME TRAINING GEN ZERS

"Trust in the LORD with all your heart,
And lean not to your own understanding;
In all your ways acknowledge Him,
And He shall direct your paths."
—(Proverbs 3:5-6 KJV)

A "trouble" so deep as to threaten the future of families, cultures and nations has gripped this nation and the West. That trouble is the national and international neglect of generations Y & Z, and those primarily engaged in their care, parents, or other caregivers. The condition has reached the extreme in many cases. As stated earlier, Barna research reports that less than 34% of our teens agree that "lying is morally wrong." Add that to a hotel sign my wife and I saw in Florida that had a large "Welcome" sign out front with smaller letters on the bottom that read, "Pets welcome – no children." I have listed below some observations about the importance of keeping the faith (see Jude 3) and passing it on to all children in our trust. As for many of our local church cultures, their church signs outside could have also read – no children (as noted by their absence inside).

1. Human parents are still God's first curriculum (see Genesis 1:26-28).

    a. He created us in His own image.
    b. Male and female created He them.
    c. Keep God's commandments in your heart (see Duet. 6:4-5).

2. Children are a gift from God.

    a. Children of every culture are a gift from God.
    b. We must bring them to fulfillment of God's design for them.
    c. We must love them.

3. Children are open to God.

    a. Children are capable of a Spiritual experience.
    b. Birth through about age 5, children experience (fantasy versus reality).
    c. They will separate with a stable environment / real faith.

4. Jesus placed a high value on children.

    a. We must accept them where they are – let them be children.
    b. Jesus changed the life molding environment.
    c. Accept them at various life stages.

5. The church is the family of God.

    a. Jesus identified His mother and brother (see Matt. 12:48-50).
    b. The congregation is the extended family.
    c. Children were created for fellowship.

6. Christianity is never more than one generation from extinction.

   a. Christianity is not according to genes, birthright, nor inheritance.
   b. We must model and share the knowledge of God with them.
   c. We must unfold the mighty acts of God – to let them see Jesus.

7. The early years set the tone for lifelong values.

   a. Invest early in every child – life experiences are profoundly shaped. Children are being taught that the shape of their life is established by the time they are five years old.
   b. Church ministries must have long range goals and early value influence.
   c. Invest energy in children for their whole life.

8. Children deserve to be helped to moral and spiritual maturity.

   a. Children pass through cognitive stages in the development of the mind.
   b. Arrested in immature levels – can fail to grow in faith and behavior.
   c. Biological versus moral development.

9. Early, consistent saturation in a warm, Christian nurturing environment helps children respond personally to Christ's (salvation).

   a. Birth to age 10 (+ or – 2) for the next age finds them too young for adults and too old to be a child.
   b. Children need early access to a positive Christian environment.

      c. Children must have a strong sense that they are loved by God and the church.

  10. The child's emerging life needs are best met in the Christian fellowship.

      a. God created humans and human relationships – discipleship.
      b. Whatever we sow we will reap.
      c. Children need that in self-realization (see Ephesians 4:24).

  11. Child development is best understood, appreciated, and ministered to, in the loving environment of the family of God.

      a. Millennials (Y's) and Gen Zers in church small group (Bible), mentoring, prayer, and discipleship ministries.
      b. Discipleship ministry awakens the moral sense of God's grace in healing and forgiveness, well ahead of Jr. Highschool.
      c. Giving the children a happy hopeful outlook.

"We have raised a generation of young people who know how to protest, but don't know how to pray."

Pastor Charlie Dates (Chicago)

TRAIN UP A CHILD

Spiritual formation starts best in the (home) and discipleship begins with the new birth experience (church). The first place our Christian faith should go to work is in the home – where the kingdom of God is the first priority. "Let the children *first* learn to show godliness to their own household and to make some return to their parents for this is pleasing in the sight of God." (1 Timothy 5:4 ESV) Emphasis added.

The living faith that is seen, practiced, and modeled in the home usually has a greater impact and influence than any other place. The work of the church is powerfully important, as it continues to reinforce that which effective spiritual parenting has presented in the home.

This consistent parent and church corporation equals the development of a strong spiritual foundation. Children model after their parents, so watching and listening by the age of five – we are told that many of their behavior patterns are life-long impacted. Sadly, many African American children are taught the Bible not as the Story of reality but only as disconnected stories, verses, and lessons to be taken randomly at will, disconnected from their context, and applied to our lives as we see fit.

Sadly, this method is all too shallow to form the framework of who we are according to God. As a result, we are producing a generation whose identities, morality, and purposes are being shaped by culture – not Christ!

The godly husband and wife will show love and tenderness toward each other and the children. Their lives are reflections of Jesus at home, and others can't help but see the difference! The family devotions is standard in the home (including single parent homes) that reflects Jesus Christ in homes. Do we really live for God at home? "For the husband is the head of the wife even as Christ is the Head of the Church, His body, and is Himself its Savior." (Ephesians 5:23 ESV)

"Children obey your parents in the Lord for this is right. 'Honor your father and mother (this is the first commandment with promise), that it may go well with you and that you may live a long life." (Ephesians 6:1-3 ESV) Emphasis added.

This is a direct command to children, to please the Lord. It is sad when children, who are professing Christians, rebel against their parents and thereby sin against Christ and the church. Christian sons and daughters should live up to their holistic, high standard in Christ as members of His body. Those of us that are His must shine (godly influence) at all times. There would be less selfishness and more love, less impatience and more kindness, less consumerism (less stuff) and more living for the things that really matters. As stated earlier, Jesus warned about causing children to sin. Most pastors and Bible teachers would agree that expository preaching, and teaching are best for giving God's whole program for humanity:

- Creation
- Redemption
- Reconciliation
- Consummation

We do not adjust the Bible to the age – but
we adjust the age to the Bible.

MARRIAGE IN THE HOME

In 1 Thessalonians 4:1-8, Paul deals with marriage in the home. The Christian has the responsibility of building a Christian home *that will glorify God,* so begin here. Immorality is basically selfishness, lust, and robbery. Therefore, Paul admonishes them to live to please God and not themselves. He had set the example (see vv. 2-4) and now he expected them to follow. He had commanded them, from the Lord, to live in holiness and purity – *by the power of God, the Holy Spirit.* God's will for them (and for us today) is that they be justified and sanctified, which means "set apart for a purpose." Emphasis added.

Rejecting **holiness** is rejecting **God** and the
ministry of the **Holy Spirit** within us.

Parental fitness

As the parents, grandparents, and significant others of the Gen Z generation, we have the daily responsibility of devoting ourselves more and more to God so that in spirit, soul, and body – we completely belong to Him (see 5:32). In a day of growing wealth, power, and relativistic philosophy, sexual immorality and perversions, murder and violence, depletion of understanding and cooperation among races, rising world economic crises, and cultural deconstruction of the foundations of truth and the moral law of God. God wants and expects obedience from those who are His!

Parents and mentors must create space for the difficult questions kids ask about God, life, and the faith. This is extremely critical not only for navigating their way through life in this information age[9] but also for motivating children to learn who they are.

Motivative action can come from three sources:

1. An awareness of the desperate condition of marriage and the family today.
2. Then there is the hungering of parents for relief.
3. Relief can be found in the gospel of Jesus Christ with generation Z, just as was the case with past generations.

SHAPING A BIBLICAL WORLDVIEW

Despite all the noise in our culture, parents remain the most important voices in the lives of their children. Isn't that good news today? And it's good to know that churches and mentors also have considerable influence. First, in the context of strong relationships we can help children form a strong, informed, and thoughtful Biblical worldview. In their book, *A Practical Guide to Culture"* John Stonestreet and Brett Kunkle (from T.S. Elliot's book) have listed five "How to" points to help children to successfully accomplish this:

---

[9] According to Wikipedia, the information age is "characterized by the shift from traditional industry ... to an economy based on information computerization.

1. Talk about worldviews early and often.
2. Explain non- biblical worldviews.
3. Strongly encourage your children to read good books.
4. Discuss ideas whenever possible.
5. Ask good questions.[10]

It has been said, worldviews are caught not taught. All of us have fundamental beliefs, whether the world just happened after a big bang and thus the world appeared. First, our worldview is the framework of our basic beliefs. We build our lives and make decisions based on these fundamental assumptions. It is necessary that we stop and examine our worldview to insure we have the right one. Our view of the world is our explanation of reality, including our beliefs about the following:[11]

- Origin: Where did all of this come from?
- Identity: What is a human being?
- Meaning: What is the meaning of life? What is our purpose?
- Morality: Who determines right and wrong? What is wrong with the world, and how can it be fixed?
- Destiny: What happens when we die?

Second, our worldview determines our view for the world. Our worldview shapes our values, and our values shape our behavior. Our actions reflect our beliefs about life. Black Gen Zers can keep their heads and hearts above the fray. They can become bold defenders of truth. The gospel of Jesus Christ has the power to save in any generation or era. We are the empowered conduits through whom the Holy Spirit can work in any place to save and help Gen Zers for the glory of God.

---

[10]   T.S. Eliot, *The Rock: A Pageant Play* (New York: Harcourt, Brace, 1934) pt. 1, lines 15-16.

[11]   John Stonestreet & Brett 2.uylukunkle, *A practical Guide to Culture* (David C. Cook publisher 2017) page 91

CHURCH IN A CLASH OF WORLDVIEWS (MODERN TO POSTMODERN)

Throughout the history of this nation, there have been glimpses of revival and awakening such as the first and second Great Awakenings, the Azusa Street Revival of 1906 in Los Angeles, (note: who was William Seymour), and the many Dr. Billy Graham evangelistic crusades just to name a few. I heard a preacher say on TV this morning that, we are now in the third Great Awakening. We are witnessing something new that has not happened since the first century. Magdalene and I have traveled, lived, and served the Lord on three continents and met people of many so-called races, nationalities, and cultures. I see something happening on a global scale. There is a shift from a modernistic worldview to a postmodern worldview.[12] Among the true born again from above believers, there is really only One Lord!

The postmodern worldview is "bad news"
for the American Church!

Now ask me why? The postmodern view is the idea that everyone can believe what they want to believe. To this view there is no such thing as absolute truth. In this worldview reality does not exist. The answers to life's questions are always changing. For example, here's a statement we all think to be true. I'm wearing a blue suit. You think that's true because the statement itself corresponds to the way things really are.

Postmodernism rejects by rejecting the concept of truth; truth now is what works for you. The truth in this worldview is not reasonable at all. What they are really against is our Truth. As stated earlier, God has given us all "freewill," but it doesn't mean all of our ideas and actions are right. Absolute truth does exist.

Evangelizing to the post-modern mind is communicating truth to someone that is not sure what truth is or if it even exists at

---

12 Accessed 10/6/22 //voices. Lifeway-com/culture-current events & how does postmodernism affect our culture today.

all – is a very difficult task. To the post-modern mind, since truth is not absolute – the spiritual absolutes that Christians hold on to, the post-modern mind insists do not exist! Here's the rub, many of our pastors, churches, and para-ministries, are not familiar with postmodernism – those of us who know the truth must share this knowledge. It has wrecked the church and the culture.

As stated, in other sections of this book, you can see proponents of this worldview working in all areas of society. Remember the Word of God is the kingdom standard for the church. Yet, I think postmodernism is enemy number one to the church today; so many are addressing the problem without the Bible, but with feelings. Can that be the reason that our church growth and attendance are waning? How is this worldview affecting your church?

A BIBLICAL WORLDVIEW

A biblical worldview must be taught, then caught! The following points form the prerequisites for a biblical worldview:

- Believe the gospel of Jesus Christ
- Believe that absolute moral truth exists.
- Believe that the Bible is totally accurate in all its principles and teachings.
- Believe that Satan is considered to be a real being, not a mere symbol.
- Believe that a person can't earn his or her way to heaven by trying to be good or doing good works.
- Believe that Jesus Christ lived a sinless life on earth.
- Believe that God is all-knowing, all-powerful Creator of the whole world and He still rules the universe today.

On a global scale, God is speaking simultaneously to a new and fresh expression of His kingdom here on the earth. I pray that every Christian longs for the spiritual experience of kingdom life as described in the Book of Acts. I am suggesting that we, Christians individually and corporately (now living in the first quarter of the Twenty-first century) have so much more opportunity for the spread of the true gospel and the kingdom than any period since the first century.

These are dark days, but darkness is – when the light shines the brightest. We (the body of Christ) must make some drastic changes in our (thinking and doing) if our light is to shine brightly in this dark world today. Listen to a timely message from my files:

Everything but God

Thousands of our parents across the land
have given their children everything
but God.
They have provided them with clothing,
good food and a liberal education,
but no Savior!
They have taken them to the movies,
but not to church.
They have read to them
"comic strips" from the Sunday papers,
but not the Bible.
They have cursed before their children,
but never have they prayed!
They live by God's goodness every day,
but not by His Gospel!
Pity such children – shame on such parents!

The window of opportunity for the people to do so, on the earth is swiftly closing!

Because a thing has been practiced daily for the past one hundred years does not mean it is right – likewise, just because a thing has not been practiced for the past one hundred years does not mean it's wrong. – Anonymous

---

It has been said, The last seven words of a dying church are, "We have never done it like that!" The home and the church must identify with this change and adapt how it presents the Gospel – or it will never be received by society.

CHANGED RULES

In our own time the covering more or less of Christianity in the Western portion of civilization has been torn open, and a flood of new structures of spiritual beliefs and practices have invaded. Many of the traditional clearly accepted structures which gave meaning to life and stability under a biblical worldview's influence in the West has been drastically changed:

- Morality has been relativized opposing personal or social convictions.
- Acceptable models of sex, marriage, and the family allow various combinations of persons and genders.
- Honesty means being loyal to one's own inner commitments more than to outside expectations or objective facts.
- Marriage and cohabitation (shacking) are mutually convenient today neither need to be based on true love or Biblical truths.
- Motherhood and abortion are celebrated in the same breath on demand.
- The meaning and context of spirituality and religion have undergone change no less fundamental.
- The idea of God now allows for polytheism (many gods) or pantheism (everything is god).

The average Black millennial in this country today no longer defines a vital spiritual life and communion with the infinite and personal Creator who is revealed in the Bible. The spirituality he or she makes may be a blend of ancient practices with modern consumerism or none at all.

I remember the fifties some call them the good old days (they were!), saint and sinner alike understood the biblical perspective consciously or unconsciously – a biblical worldview consisting of fundamental ideas – about God, morality, sexuality, family, marriage, motherhood, spirituality, and religion. African Americans were just as sinful and suffered just as many problems due to privilege, systemic and institutional racism, and sexism.

Yet, the consistent biblical view existed. A couple of years ago, it was determined that the Jewish experience (the Holocaust) of World War II Germany has caused generational trauma (damage) to the Jewish people in every generation to this day. Likewise, we don't need the social scientists to determine generational trauma (damage) from institutional slavery's effect on every African American throughout their life in every generation since the first arrivals.

I have observed this transformation from different countries of the world over a period of time. I have preached and lectured extensively on it and have authored books about it. It is my prayer that by God's grace, this reflection will allow the churches success in analyzing what is happening today and what true Christians [God's remnant] everywhere, who are called to be salt and light in this dark world can go about it. In spite of all we've been through and are presently experiencing, the goal remains, to preach the gospel clearly in our day and bless the culture with our God-honoring life of witness for the Glory of God. Give them Jesus!

WHAT DID WE LEAVE THEM?

As I pointed out in an earlier section, the changed culture in which we are now living is the only culture our young Millennials, and Gen Zers, and other young people have known. However, a lack of knowledge about the recent past is creating many problems for them. Many Black pastors are as frustrated as the Millennials (individuals born between 1980 and 2000) are increasingly disinterested in traditional church experiences.

Despite our best programming and outreach efforts many churches have been unable to attract, retain, and spiritually develop a substantial number of this generation. Certainly, with the present-day state of their congregations many church leaders find themselves in a state of bereavement. They are grieving the perceived loss of the church's youth, vitality, and in some cases even the church's relevance in this strange new digital world.

For many congregations who are having trouble attracting and developing this next generation of the church, are also wondering can we survive and thrive the next 10 or 20 years? Then there are some churches that were on life-support before the COVID – lockdown and have turned in their keys. Thinking that we have failed them, many Gen Y and Gen Zers are like a person drowning, grasping for any and everything to help them. Current generations are accepting contemporary religious beliefs, and lifestyle choices as *normal* without realizing just how *abnormal* they were *just* a few years ago!

Sadly, both young and old Christians may seek wisdom uncritically from the surrounding culture, whose assumptions and values are often decidedly un-Christian. Jay Leach

---

While we should desire to understand our culture in order to bear witness to Jesus in it, however, it is imperative that we *avoid conforming* to its expectations just to receive its affirmation! One of the most important responsibilities of the church is to call ourselves and all of the cultures in every generation to the rule that judges all other rules – that rule is the rule of faith – the Word of God!

THE BIG "LIE"

No matter how bad things may be getting in this country and the world, God is still in charge of the whole universe. What we are experiencing, and seeing come to past before our very eyes daily was prophesied in the Bible 2000 years ago. In fact, the truths prophesied in the Bible concerning today's events and attitudes would shock the world for their accuracy.

The devil and his appointees work overtime every day trying to keep the truth covered over from the people of the world. God instituted His universal program long before He created angel or man. However, God created all spirit beings (angelic or human) with a free-will – rather than robotized.

One of the angels He created named Lucifer chose to exercise his free-will and rebelled against God rather than to worship, love, honor, and glorify Him. We find Lucifer's dreams and aspirations (five "I will") recorded in Isaiah 14:13-14, so *here* we have the answer many ask, "where did the devil come from?"

For thou hast said in thine heart,

- *I will ascend into heaven,*
- *I will exalt my throne above the stars of God:*
- *I will sit also upon the mount of the congregation; in the* sides *of the north:*
- *I will ascend above the heights of the clouds;*
- *I will be like the Highest.*

Just as Jesus is the personification of **truth** – so the devil is the personification the **lie**. Jesus said of the devil,

"Ye are of your father the devil, and the lusts of your father ye will do. He was a murderer from the beginning, and abode not in the truth, because there is no truth in him. When he speaketh of his own: for he is a liar, and the father of it." (John 8:44 KJV)

Prior to Lucifer's rebellion there was only one will, God's will." The big lie is, "I don't need God." I can handle my life without Him. This is the mindset of the blinded unsaved person. He or she probably doesn't know any better, but today, so many people including some nominal and carnally minded Christians are saying the same thing about God.

People see evidence of the true God in creation, but then they *choose* to become blind!

"What can be known of God is manifest in them, for God has shown it to them. For since the creation of the world His invisible attributes are clearly seen, being understood by the things that are made, even His eternal power and Godhead, so that they are without excuse." (Romans 1:19-20 NKJV)

The human mind, even in its fallen state, is capable of amazing intellectual constructs but also of irrational conclusions that dehumanize culture. This is not simply irrational and inconsistent; it is dishonest. The *Lie will always contradict itself.* Pontius Pilate declared Jesus's innocence three times before having Him flogged and *crucified.*

Without God, man is incapable of "sound judgment." A quick survey of all of our nation's institutions and systems will attest to that fact. Everywhere you turn there is disfunction, decay, desolation, and the "Big Lie," because of man's lack of wisdom, and poor reasoning – this is the state of all people who *reject* the knowledge of God. Because, although they knew:

- They did not glorify Him as God,
- They were not thankful,
- They became futile in their thoughts,
- And their foolish hearts (v. 21).

*"Professing to be wise, they became fools, and changed the glory of incorruptible God into <u>an **image** made like a corruptible man</u> – and birds and four-footed animals and creeping things."* (vv. 22-23 NKJV) Emphasis added throughout.

GOD'S RIGHTEOUS JUDGMENT

Therefore, God gave them up to uncleanness, in the lusts of their hearts, to <u>dishonor their bodies</u> among themselves, who exchanged <u>the truth of God for a lie,</u> and worshipped and served <u>the creature rather than the Creator,</u> who is blessed forever. Amen (vv. 24-25 NKJV)

For this reason, "God gave them up to *vile passions.* For even their women exchanged the natural use for what is against nature. Likewise, also the men, leaving the natural use of the woman, burned in their lust for one another, men with men committing what is shameful, and receiving in themselves the penalty of their error which was due." (vv. 26-27 NKJV)

God gave them over to a debased mind

And even as they did not like to retain God in their knowledge, God gave them over to a *debased mind*, to do those things which are not fitting; being filled with:

- all unrighteousness
- sexual immorality
- wickedness
- covetousness
- maliciousness
- full of envy
- murder
- strife
- deceit
- evil-mindedness
- they are whisperers
- backbiters
- haters of God
- violent
- proud
- boasters
- inventors of evil things
- disobedient to parents
- undiscerning
- untrustworthy
- unloving
- unforgiving spirit
- unmerciful

Who knowing the *righteous judgment of God,* that those who *practice* such things are deserving of death, not only do the same but also approve of those who practice them. (vv. 28-32 NKJV)

The verses above contain one of the most extensive lists of sins in all Scripture. The list shows the broad sweep of human depravity (compare **all** in v. 29). Please note, that while society tends to rationalize certain sins – God judges *all* sin. These sins particularly reveal our rebellious hearts. All without exception, deserves God's punishment (study prayerfully Romans 3:22-23; 6:19-23).

In 1:29-32, Paul declares that all unrighteous people are without excuse. Additionally, he exposes the self-righteous (those who judge others) are inexcusable, by revealing the standards by which everyone will be judged. Judgment will be:

1. according to truth (verses 1-5)
2. according to works (verses 6-11)
3. according to the light one has of God's Word (vv. 12-16)

SHATTERED

Dr. Tony Evans, founder, and senior pastor of Oak Cliff Bible Fellowship in Dallas, TX, has a way of expressing truth that is very memorable. In a sermon he preached about the ripple effect that selfish or sinful individuals will produce in the wider society if you are messed up:

> If you're a messed-up man and you have a family, you're going to help make a messed-up family.
>
> If you're a messed-up man contributing to a messed-up family, and your messed-up family goes to church, then you have a messed-family's gonna make its contribution to a messed-up church ......
>
> If you're a messed-up man contributing to a messed-up family resulting in a messed-up church causing a messed-up neighborhood, and your neighborhood's part of a city, well, now your messed-up neighborhood's gonna make its contribution to a messed-up city ....
>
> If you're a messed-up man contributing to a messed-up family resulting in a messed-up church causing a messed-up neighborhood that resides in a messed-up city that's part of a messed-up county, and your county's part of the state, well, now, your

messed-up county's gonna make its contribution to a messed-state.

If you're a messed-up man contributing to a messed-up family resulting in a messed-up church causing a messed-up neighborhood that resides in a messed-up city that's part of a messed-up county contributing to a messed-state, and your state's part of the country, well, now your messed-up state's gonna make its contribution to a messed-up nation.

If you're a messed-up man contributing to a messed-up family resulting in a messed-up church causing a messed-up neighborhood that resides in a messed-up city that's part of a messed-up county that's contributing to a messed-up state that's contributing to a messed-up country, and your country's part of the world, well now your messed-up country is gonna make its contribution to a messed-world.[13]

The progression Dr. Evans describes here is the same as Paul's in 2 Timothy 3:1-5, describing the *selfishness* of the end time people:

"This know also, in the last days perilous times shall come. For men shall be lovers of their own selves, covetous, boasters, proud, blasphemers, disobedient to parents, unthankful, unholy,' without natural affection, trucebreakers, false accusers, incontinent, fierce, despisers of those that are good, 'traitors, heady, high-minded, lovers of pleasures more than lovers of God; having a form of godliness but denying the power thereof: from such turn away." (2 Timothy 3:1-5 KJV)

The more broken the families present in a society, the more broken that society will become.

---

[13] Tony Evans, "Why Men Matter," *Tony Evans The Urban Alternative*, April 1, 2021, http://tonytevens.org/podcast/why-men-matter-part-1/; https//tonyevans.org/podcast/why-men-matter-part-2/.

STUDY GUIDE : WORKSHEET & REFLECTIONS CHAPTER 3

1. A trouble so deep as to threaten the future of the family, cultures and nations is national and international _____ of generation Y and Z.

2. Children are a gift _____ _____.

3. Christianity is never more than _____ generation from _____.

4. Early consistent _____ of the Word of God, in a warm, Christian nurturing _____ helps children to respond personally to Christ's salvation.

5. Despite all the noise in the culture, _____ the most important voices in the _____ of their children.

6. Explain the "Big Lie" in the space below.

7. Morality has been _____ opposing personal or social convictions.

Chapter Four

IT'S MORE THAN A GENERATIONAL GAP

"Another generation grew up
who knew neither the LORD
nor what He had done for Israel."

Judges 2:10 ESV

One day while meeting with the Board of Deacons to discuss the loss of most of their youth and young adults; the pastor asked the deacons what should we do to retain and train our Millennials and Gen Zers? One of the older deacons rose and said, of the wondering youths and young adults, "I'm telling you; these generations are no different than when I was a teenager or when I went to college." It is the same thing with young people today. "When I was in high school, I experimented with alcohol, rebelled, and rejected church. But then I got older. I got married and when we had kids, I returned to my roots and came back to church."

Then he grinned, as if his case had been clearly made. "It's the same thing with young people today. They are just like I was. One day they're all gonna grow up and come back to church.' All of this is simply a generation-gap issue." The pastor sat patiently and when he finished, he said, "You said you had kids and returned to your roots." "Yep," he answered, "just like they will when they get older and come back to church."

"What if by their roots they were never involved in church or the Christian faith to begin with? What if the roots they put down while growing up were a pluralistic mix of world faiths, leaning toward more of an Eastern philosophy? How can they return to their roots of church and Christianity if they don't have any roots there to return to?

After a brief pause, he is looking puzzled later he said, "I don't know what they will do then." Earlier, in American church history, this would have been right. Yet, many pastors and other church leaders especially in traditional churches agree with the deacon. But in recent years, these young people have grown up in a world of post-modernism, post-Christian values and perspectives. They simply have no Christian roots to turn to!

In Judges 2:10 we find a time when *"another generation grew up, who knew neither the LORD nor what He had done for Israel."* If this could be done in ancient Israel, where God was such a central and visible part of the culture – couldn't that be happening in our country and churches today? Many of our smaller churches in America are really going through some unexplainable situations today following the COVID shut down and trying to reopen and operate under the old paradigm. Many continue to believe, speak, and lead from the perspective and mindset of the deacon mentioned in the beginning of this section.

BORN IN AMERICA

In the modern era (A.D. 1500 – 2000) a person raised in America (after the nation's birth) would receive a primary Judeo-Christian upbringing. For the most part, in the modern era, everyone grew up in an atmosphere that taught the values of the Judeo-Christian faith.

Even if one was not a Christian, he or she:

- probably agreed with most biblical values and ethics

- tried to live by the Ten Commandments
- understood many of the basic Bible stories
- knew what it meant that Jesus died for sins
- "God" meant the Judeo-Christian God

A person would grow by taking on the traits of the modern era

- Including monotheism (belief in one God)
- A rational, logical system of learning
- Religion was good during modern times
- A modern person learned propositionally
- Able to understand and master concepts by breaking them down into systems
- Most people didn't travel a lot and viewed life through a hometown lens
- Truth was knowable and absolute
- The Bible, for most people, provided a reference point for all experience
- It told the story of where life came from, its purpose, and its meaning.

What is it like growing up in a post-Christian era with a postmodern atmosphere and postmodern cultural traits?

- In the post-Christian era (beginning A.D. 2000), the values and beliefs of a person raised in America are shaped by a global, pluralistic atmosphere.
- This person has instant exposure to global news, global fashions, global music, and global religions.
- There are many gods, many faiths, many forms of spiritual expression from which to choose.
- In a postmodern atmosphere a person grows up learning that all faiths are equal, but that Christianity is primarily a negative religion, known for finger-pointing and condemning the behavior of others.
- Here the Ten Commandments are not taught, and the Bible is simply one of many religious writings.

- Ethics and morals are based on personal choice, as families encourage their children to make their own decisions about religion and to be tolerant of all beliefs.
- As truth is denied, therapy remains the question here, moved from "what's true?" to "what makes me feel good."
- There are public celebrations of all lifestyles as equal. "Homophobia" is now targeted as the "real sin" and demands tolerance of alternative lifestyles.
- Post Christian era refuses to be instructed and bound by the biblical text.
- Many churches have chosen to "go along" in order to "get along."
- The issues of moral concern end up in many cases solved around the "self."
- A major influence on a postmodern person's ethics and morals is what they learn from the media and what is accepted by their peers.
- Although relativism is more of a postmodern world, most agree on some absolutes, such as the wrongness of violence, murder, or like the evil of 9/11.
- In a post-Christian world, pluralism is the norm. Buddhism, Wicca, Christianity, Islam, Hinduism, or an eclectic blend, are all a part of the soil.
- The basis of learning has shifted from logic and rational, systemic thought to the realm of experience.
- People long for the mystical and the spiritual rather than the evidential and fact-based faith of the modern era.23
- The way people think is more fluid than systematic, more global, than local, more communal than individualistic.
- And to postmodernism a high value is placed on personal preference and choice, as opposed to predetermined truth.

TRUST IN INSTITUTIONS

Trust in institutions – corporate, government, education, and even religious institutions – has dropped tremendously. Younger generations are trying to create accountability structures that are not corporate in nature. What does decentralized mission and ministry look like? How could it work? How could it work? These are crucial questions.

In an earlier section, I mentioned the fact that a small group Bible study or food give-away would be to the liking of Gen Zers than tied down in a three piece business suit as a spectator in in the pew during weekly traditional 11 a.m. Sunday worship service. Those persons born between 1900 and 1945 normally remained at one job for decades then retire. At the same time if you were a Christian, you belonged to the same denomination, even though you moved to another city. You were loyal to brands and organizations for life.

TRUST CERTAIN PEOPLE

If you were born from the late 1940s up until the early 1980s, your generation witnessed a shift away from loyalty to an institution because too many leaders failed morally or financially. The emerging generations at the time found it safer to become committed to certain individuals they trusted over the larger organizations.

Those emerging of age during those years saw failed leadership in the politics of Vietnam, the Watergate scandal, the Iran hostage rescue, and people of faith. I became a pastor in 1980, the older generation at the time really grieved over the loss of their children and grandchildren once they left home for college or the world.

Many of the young people began to change their faith and a greater number became non-affiliated (nones). Of course I had no idea of what was going on. I never heard it discussed in Bible College and that coupled 26.5 years of active duty in the U.S. Army. I didn't have a ready answer for them. Of course, it didn't take a genius to see what was going on. With the land being swallowed up by the housing industry and larger farmers, they were witnessing the close of an era.

TRUST IN IDEAS

The years between 1985 and 2020 has seen so much failed leadership and having witnessed the stories of their failure in the media, the emerging generations shifted their loyalties to ideas. The Y and Z generations preferred to follow ideals rather than to follow a *single* leader.

A 2021 Barna Research Group survey of Generation Z uncovered that while most Gen Zers feel supported by older generations, nearly two-thirds (64 percent) seek advice from their peers – not their elders. In an earlier section, I mentioned that we elders can learn from the younger generations – as well as teach them.

DIVERSITY?

Thankfully, workplace diversity expectations among Gen Zers are clearly different than older ones. Younger generations tend to think that racial justice matters within their own control and culture. Their view of systemic racism incorporates how the place of employment makes decisions on diversity and how power is shared. Sadly, young Gen Zers and the older tend to view this issue differently. Nearly half of Black and Hispanic employees and job seekers said they had quite a job after experiencing discrimination at work. The nation is clearly divided, and millions are not sure who to trust.

STUDY GUIDE: WORKSHEET AND REFLECTIONS
CHAPTER 4

1. A trouble so deep as to threaten the future of the family, cultures and nations is national and international *neglect* of generation Y and Z.

2. Children are a gift from _____.

3. Children are capable of a _____ experience.

4. Christianity is never more than _____ generation from _____.

5. Early consistent saturation of the Word of God, in a warm, Christian nurturing environment helps children respond personally to Christ's salvation.

6. Despite all the noise of in the culture, parents remain the most important voices in the lives of their children.

7. Morality has been _____ opposing personal or social convicTIONS.

Chapter Five

CHANGE THE CULTURE

"Do not be conformed to this world, but be transformed by the renewal of your mind, that by testing you may discern what is the will of God, what is good and acceptable and perfect." (Romans 12:2 ESV)

In the western world culture, we frequently hear someone speaking about the empty nest syndrome which is the feeling of grief and loneliness parents experience when their adult children leave home. The church version has been called the empty "net" syndrome, the disappointment we feel when we lose our young adults to go into the world.

I am concerned about *filling the **net*** with the unchurched, de-churched and the churched, especially Millennials and Gen Zers. If we keep our course and don't recognize this issue by making the *necessary changes* in our church culture, we can be sure we will lose our future. A special thought for all local churches, since the de-churched have emerged as a special problem for the churches. In his book *Church Refugees,* John Packard, PH.D. mentioned some tensions that arose therein:

- They wanted community ... and got judgment.
- They wanted to affect the life of the church ... and got bureaucracy.

- They wanted conversation ... but got doctrine.
- They wanted meaningful engagement with the world ... and got moral prescription.[14]

Research shows that the de-churched phenomenon is directly attributable to a pattern that exists in leadership structures and church cultures – resistance to (any) changes (downplays innovation) in most denominations and local churches across the United States.

THE MISSING LINK

Today, the church is suffering from not being able to keep new converts, and that is tragic, but what is worse – we are not retaining third and fourth generation believers either; indicating that we are *not* carrying out the "teaching them all" part of the command of Christ, Himself in the (make disciples) mission of Matthew 28:19-20.

The greatest or first change we should make is four-fold to go back to the Bible, revive prayer ministry in our churches, welcome the Holy Spirit and His gifts and ministries (back within us) and in the churches – and hear Him! Unfortunately, it's easier to tell people what is wrong with them than it is to disciple them into wholeness. Practical discipleship begins immediately after being born again. Only a disciple can make a disciple by teaching survival between the two advents.

In our church culture today, we act as if there are certain experts who engage this great task – but the Bible teaches that *all believers* in the body of Christ are expected to love, care about, be concerned for, and show compassion to those outside of the faith through gospel witness. All Christians must know Christ and their Bible intimately!

This generation is not going to do something
just because you tell them.

---

[14] Packard, Josh, *Church Refuges*: Sociologists reveal why people are DONE with church but not their faith (p. 28). Group Publishing Inc., Kindle Edition.

Neither the millennial generation (Gen Y's born 1980 -2000) nor (Gen Zers born 2000-2020?) responds to "because I said so." In this Information Age, we can't just tell people, "Because I said so" and then call them rebellious if they don't *blindly conform*. If you are going to deal fairly with this generation, sometimes even if your argument trumps theirs – biblically, or theoretically, let them breathe. Give them some space, the goal is preserving the relationship rather than proving the person wrong. If you win the argument and lose the person – you lost.

One reason the millennials and Gen Zers don't listen to us is because we don't listen to them. With all the information out there, everybody is talking – but few are listening. These are the young people in our church culture, that (we claim) allow for healthy, and honest conversations.

We need to remember that both evangelism and discipleship are for the inside of the church as well as the outside. Evangelism is not just winning the lost, but also for winning the found! Like the early church we must begin inside our own Jerusalem (our families, friends and loved ones) before heading off to Judea, Samaria, and the uttermost, but notice what was promised, "But ye shall receive *power* after that the Holy Ghost is come upon you …" (see Acts 1:8 KJV) The critical situation in many of our churches today is due to this [lack of power] because of voluntary disobedience. As stated throughout this book – if we are not in the Spirit, then we are striving to function in the flesh. No flesh shall inherit the kingdom.

"What are we gaining, if we convert sinners – but the world converts our young people?"

We have got to fill the gaps:

- Thus, we must first understand this *new* generation and how they think.
- Consider the options and resources we have to reach them.
- Commit to a course of action that transforms our church culture.

Now let me be clear, this is about changing our attitudes, behavior, and methodology – not changing God's message to us, (the Holy Bible).

A MINISTRY CHANGE (MODERN TO POSTMODERN)

It has been said, "the church usually lags about 40 years behind each major cultural shift. There is an ongoing *shift* in worldview. The church *must* realize this change and adapt how it presents its message – or let me be clear, the Gospel will not be heard by a disinterested society. Postmodernism, which came about during the sixties in an environment of destabilizing technological and social change. Its thinkers argue that so-called national modernism had lied to us, having told us that the human mind could (through science and reason) solve all our problems. Notice, at the center of this secular *humanistic* worldview is the human being.

In the 1960's President Lyndon B. Johnson, as part of his "Great Society" *promised* that "poverty" would be done away within his generation, well President Johnson and his generation are gone. Here we are – with more poverty than ever. Modern science *promised* that we can eliminate all diseases just as *we* did smallpox.

Today the COVID epidemic is still alive in America and the World. Smallpox is on the rebound; Monkey Pox is moving toward being a widespread concern. A new children's virus, RSV, which the news folk have called the "perfect storm" according to them has practically filled children's hospitals across this nation, along with mental health incursions running rampart.

As I stated earlier, modernism failed and therefore, being a part of modernism, which failed makes my generation failures, so the change to the *postmodern* generation follows us. If we are going to win Gen Zers to Christ, we had better learn something about their differences and our own. The emerging postmodern world lacks some definition seemingly like some politicians, because it is more a reaction *against the old worldview* than a proactive solution however, it has some inherent values that presents great opportunity for the

Good News of God's kingdom. As it stands today, much of the Black Church is quite threatened by the *shift* of postmodernity.

Perhaps another reason the Black church may be threatened by postmodernism is the fact that in many ways it is really the product of modernism. We have thought that education was our salvation; which led to the notion the more we educate people the better the world will be – which is really a modern assumption.

God's kingdom is neither modern nor postmodern. However, His kingdom can flourish in both at the same time. Within every person and in each culture as a whole are two conflicting realities: the image of God and the ugliness of sin.

Mission or the men

During my years in the Army, during "modern and postmodern times," the priority was always the mission first. Every person was valued by how helpful they were to completion of the mission. An old up front saying to the troops was, "I'm not here to win a popularity contest." In conjunction with the mission, we were expendable. Every leader had a personal mission statement. The postmodernist values *relationship* more than *mission*.

The postmodernist values *relationship* more than the *mission*.

Again, relationship is the strongest of values in the postmodern mind and heart, and it dictates the other values. Take for example truth is relative to postmodern people, most often because they value relationships with all kinds of people and don't want to exclude any. Mission is still important to the postmodern, but because they value relationships so highly, lying about who you really are is deception (hypocritical). Authenticity is valued very highly.

PASSING DOWN THE FAITH

The responsibility for passing down the faith from one generation to the next is always on the predecessor, not the successor. As parents, pastors, and other church leaders it is imperative that we gain an understanding of Millennials and Gen Zers so that we can effectively watch (over) and lead them – and not push them away. Our churches must realize that one size does not necessarily fit all.

If what we are doing is not working and we know it – should we continue to do it – and worse continue to pass it down to the next generation? Jay Leach

---

Of course, none of this can be accomplished in the "flesh," our own natural abilities (science and reason) failed in modernism. We need to ask God, the Holy Spirit for guidance and wisdom to reach, teach, and retain them within the New Covenant pattern of the early apostolic church. When my wife, Magdalene and I planted the Bread of Life Ministries Int'l Headquartered in Whiteville, North Carolina in the fall of 1998, [little millennial had reached the age of 18 and baby Gen Zers were soon to arrive in 2000].

I realized that *times had significantly changed* – in both secular culture, and church culture – from when our beloved planters and pastors first pioneered many years ago. Of course, there are basic foundational truths about God, Christ, the Gospel of Jesus Christ, the Holy Spirit and born from above believers that never changes. Biblical principles and God's moral laws *never* change!

The Word of God (the Bible), a biblical worldview, the necessity of prayer, discipling, fasting, preaching, teaching, planning, and personal witnessing, are required. In all these things relying on the Holy Spirit's presence, and power within us activated in apostolic patterns of spiritual growth to maturity, as outlined in the New Testament. The Gospel of Jesus Christ works in every era, in any place, to any people – therefore the Millennials or Gen Zers are not exceptions:

> We *will not* adjust the Bible to the Age – but
> we *will adjust* the Age to the Bible.

PASTOR CHARLES SPURGEON

The question we must ask is, *how do we reach the next generation?*

To answer that question:

- We must observe the culture in which we live and try to view the world through their eyes.
- If we are going to lead them effectively, we must first do the necessary work needed to understand why they think the way they think, or we will just become more frustrated or worse – and place the blame on them.
- Again, the responsibility of passing down the faith to the next generation is always on the predecessor, not the successor. Elijah had to *connect* with Elisha [in Elisha's own environment] and prepare him to catch the mantle.

Millennials are not leaving our churches because of our vision, or lack thereof, but because of our church *culture*. Sadly, they are departing because of the way we do things, not for the truth we believe. As a matter of course, we always assume they leave for other movements because our rules are too strict, or our standards of holiness are too ridged.

Often their claim is the church is too legalistic with a "one strike you're out" mentality, people will leave for other places where there is more grace – and less fear about sharing their struggles. Most congregations are aware of the need to reach and retain Millennials for the spiritual benefit of their souls and propagations of the gospel to future generations. However, reaching and retaining a new generation – depends on what kind of culture we are building. The truth is we are either building a church culture that draws or one that repels.

Much of the contemporary church today is buying into a *new emerging Christianity*; in which postmodern culture is tolerant, but actually producing narrow-thinking people in both the secular and much of church culture, all locked into the tight package dealing with the new tolerance. The proper knowledge as God would have it encourages students and other believers to examine all the claimants to *truth* and sort out the genuine from the false through application of the Word of God, absolute, and unchanging – the ultimate reality. So, reaching and retaining a new generation – depends on what kind of church culture and structure we are building.

If we want to see our kids rise above all the rhetorical noises, and live well in this culture, just talking about it won't get the job done. Discernment is mandatory. Young people must develop the ability to not only recognize *the truth* but also to see all of life through *the truth* – as a lens by which they identify and evaluate every idea they encounter.

Our worldview is "the framework of basic beliefs we have, whether we realize it or not, that shapes our view of the world." One writer compared a worldview with a pair of prescription eyeglasses, our worldview will either help us to see the world as it is or, if the prescription is wrong, it will keep us from seeing properly. Remember we don't look at our worldview we look through it and our view of the world is our explanation of reality to include our beliefs concerning:

- Origins: Where did it all come from?
- Identity: What is a human being?
- Meaning: What is the meaning of life?
- Morality: Who determines right and wrong?
- Destiny: What happens when we die?[15]

SURRENDER OR DISOBEY

What citizens sometimes have to do for civic or political reasons – Christians must sometimes do for spiritual or moral reasons. For both at times defiance may be the only option available.

---

[15] W. Gary Phillips, William E. Brown, and John Stonestreet, *Making Sense of Your World: A Biblical Worldview, 2nd ed.* (Salem, WI: Sheffield, 2008), 86.

We see the struggle for democracy played out daily by the people of Ukraine, through television news or other social media. Words that use to be heard and taught such as regeneration, transformation, rapture, the Tribulation, War of Armageddon, the Thousand-year Reign of Christ are spoken of in whispers or not at all.

It is in an atmosphere such as we are seeing in Eastern Europe that World Wars I and II were born. The prince of this world is hurriedly at work, and Christians the world over should know that the end times are here. In light of these things – can it be that Generation Z is the revelation generation?

What people don't want to talk about and certainly the average person, don't want to see has played out over the past number of months as observed, millions of people, much of that number, children (since March 2022). People uprooted from their homeland, homes, and families with just the clothes on their backs, husbands kissing their wives and children goodbye and then returning to the battle – these refugees many sleeping by the side of the roads, or wherever, without shelter from the winter elements, as a godless, frustrated Russian president watches his unscrupulous planning and manipulation go down the drain. Today, December 25th in the 9th month of the fighting with possible escalation always over the horizon. Read the story of David and Goliath in 1 Samuel 17 in the Bible. Do you think God is not there with David? Note the outcome!

At the beginning, stories came out of Russian missiles fired but disappearing in flight, and we saw, the largest army assembled in Europe since WWII with a 40-mile-long convoy (trucks, tanks, large-motorized artillery pieces, and missile launchers bogged down in the mud, slush, crowded rural roads, narrow city streets, and untrained Russian troops – falling prey to a determined people who have chosen death over puppetry under a dictator (i.e., David and Goliath).

While many don't want to watch all of this play out before the whole world by TV and other social media. As spiritual conditions the people and Christianity continue going downhill in this country it's so easy to just change the channel. There are many Christian leaders in this country, who continue to call the United States a Christian nation. Yet, our citizenry stand ready to pay any amount to see all the man-made destruction, blood, and gore, muck, and mire that Hollywood make happen in movies for our amusement and entertainment. As a combat Vietnam veteran, I pray much for the people of this nation, as many never imagine the possibility of such horror, and sorrow, through selfishness could so easily be produced in this country. Disaster after disaster is happening. Christian means Christ-like. Is America really Christ-like? Is America in the image of Christ? At the birth of America church attendance (100%) was mandatory. Today church attendance has dropped to less than 37%. Research shows that at its birth America was a Christian nation but has been on a constant decline ever since.

I fear that the visual imagery of war-torn Ukraine, poverty-stricken Haiti with murderous gangs pillaging and terrorizing their own neighborhoods, and the fear and suffering of those who are [always] the most vulnerable and innocent in any such scenario [the elderly, women, and children, sick]. These scenes flashing across TV's and other social media are not registering in our consciousness as they should. Could it be that we think America is above that? Can one person or group cause such suffering in this country? However, we know that sooner or later, Christians the world-over will be required to *bow the knee* once again to a new Caesar – Antichrist. In Revelation 20:4, we read,

"And I saw thrones, and they sat on them, and judgment was committed to them. Then I saw the souls of those who had been beheaded for their witness to Jesus and for the Word of God, who had not worshipped the beast or his image, and had not received his mark on their foreheads or on their hands. And they lived and reigned with Christ for a thousand years." (NKJV)

In the David narrative before, notice, King Saul and the Army of Israel stood frozen in fear, with all eyes on the giant, Goliath. David seeing the opportunity, seized the moment *in the name of the Lord,* and killed Goliath. See the rest of the story! David's eyes were on God, whom he loved and faithfully served. Here we can readily see that size bears little relationship to significance with God, our Creator. How big is your God? In recent decades, we have seen the gradual moral deterioration of the foundational underpinnings of this nation – and it is not all surprising, as humanity *naturally tilts* toward *depravity* and self-destruction. Three of Armageddon's main players are warming up together in the bull pen China, Russia, and Iran (see Ezekiel 38 and 39).

But Satan is also pushing his own end-times agenda, since he knows he has but a short time – and he is using *governments* to achieve his goal; as time passes the coronavirus, and now the Ukraine war; it is apparent that there is a growing sentiment toward (globalism) and a one-world government, coupled with a deceptively tempting submission to federal mandates – we find ourselves sliding back toward Babylon and *into the era of Antichrist.*

The initial platform of this final world government will be built upon a false "peace" and "safety" (see 1 Thessalonians 5:3; also, Daniel 9:27; Revelation 6:2) but will soon turn to tyranny and dictatorial domination (see Revelation 13:14-17). There has been much speculation through the years concerning which countries will be a part of that federation. Today we are seeing several simultaneous attempts at unifying the Gentile nations over shared causes, and for the so-called common good of mankind.

The COVID-19 epidemic of 2020 was not the first such plague to threaten planet Earth. Throughout history, widespread death and destruction going back to biblical times, including the judgment that devastated Egypt and Pharoah of 185,000 lives in one night. Plagues, and pestilences are found throughout the Bible. The Spanish Flu of the last century brought death to as many as 50 million worldwide.

Then more recently, HIV/AIDS has taken 35 million lives since making its first appearance in 1981. By June 2020, more than eight million cases of COVID were reported in some 200 countries. But according to the Book of Revelation, these pestilences will not be the last *nor* the deadliest.

The great loss of lives was not the only tragedy as the result of the epidemic. Many world leaders began viewing the pandemic as great opportunity to sound *calls for global unity.* In the midst of the outbreak, former secretary-general of the United Nations Ban Ki-moon of South Korea cited the pandemic was in every corner of the world; and therefore, his solution was for each country to begin developing a "global governance system" led by the U.N. that would address this international crisis.

Such operations have been in the news lately, the G7, the G20, and of course the European Union, which is presently made up of 27 countries. It is unclear what the precise positions of nations will be at the time of the Antichrist's appearance.

However, what we do know is that Antichrist's empire will be represented by ten kings or nations (see Revelation 13:1; 17:3, 12-13). Whatever the situation may be, the most dominant expression of the empire will be seen during the second half of the seven-year tribulation period (see Daniel 9:24).

THE REBIRTH OF BABYLON

The headquarters for the new world order will be in Babylon. Babylon, the former leader of the ancient world, will once again be a great religious and commercial city-system. The apostle John pictured Babylon as a prostitute riding on the back of the beast (Antichrist). Study prayerfully and carefully, Revelation 17-18.

The immoral woman, the religion of Babylon, will seduce and intoxicate the people of Earth with her apostate religion. The fact that she rides on top of the beast signifies that she will not only be supported by the Antichrist but will also initially overshadow him in some way. There are some men and women in our government at every level who have sworn allegiance not only on a Bible but also to the principles found therein. Yet, evil forces in the present darkness are also fighting with tremendous zeal and passion to achieve their godless, and immoral agenda.

This is not only true of the ultra-left liberal who are determined to eradicate Christians and Christianity – but also it applies to a growing louder ultra-right anarchist attitude and movement that – is determined to destroy our Democracy. There is an increasingly bolder decay in the realm of politics, which, means any truly Biblical Christian appointee will in all probability be brutally opposed and vilified in an effort to keep him or her from holding public office.

THE LIGHT OF THE WORLD

As Christians, we must remind ourselves that it is *the Church,* **not** government, that is responsible for having a *positive moral influence* on <u>culture and restraining evil.</u> When we put our trust in leaders who are sympathetic to Christian beliefs, we often relax, back off, and hand the reins to them. However,

- God never said to the government, "You are the light of the world," He said that to us, "born from above believers" (Matthew 5:14).
- He never described government as being "the pillar in support of truth, "but Scripture portrays the church in that manner" (see 1 Timothy 3:15).
- The church must recognize that *no* president or no administration can save us – "only God can do that."

A Christian-friendly leader or any other government official sympathetic to Christian values is definitely an asset, however, we must remember that a Christian-friendly leader can only wage a political or legal war against; satanically inspired evil. No matter how good and effective human government is it still really has no bearing on God's eternal kingdom.

Government does affect our lives, but it does not, and it cannot hinder the gospel, for the Word of God is not imprisoned (see 2 Timothy 2:9). And the kingdom agenda we preach and promote "is not of this world" (see John 18:36).

If past prophetic previews are any indication, in the days leading up to the *rapture,*[16] humanity will experience a *gradual conditioning* toward a herd mentality – where individual rights are eroded and replaced with governmental overreach.

---

[16] RAPTURE: A popular term used with reference to the resurrection and translation of the saints, John 14:3; 1 Cor. 15:51, 52; Phil. 3:20,21; 1 Thess. 3:13; 4:13-18. The word comes from a Latin word meaning to seize or to snatch and is a synonym for translation. Associated with that are exhortations to waiting, 1 Thess. 1:10; watching, 1 Thess. 5:6, looking for the blessed hope, Titus M2:13, loving His appearing, 2 Tim. 4:8, putting one another in remembrance, 1 Tim. 4:6 and Heb. 10:25. (Nave's Topical Bible, Moody Press, Chicago, 1974). 1028

So, whatever we are witnessing of this in our culture today will grow worse according to the Scripture. In 2 Timothy 3:1-7, Paul warns the church corporately and individually, "This know also, that in the last days perilous times shall come."

"For men shall be,

- Lovers of their own selves
- Covetous
- Boasters
- Proud
- Blasphemers
- Disobedient to parents
- Unthankful
- Unholy
- Without natural affection
- Trucebreakers
- False accusers
- Incontinent
- Fierce
- Despisers of those that are good
- Traitors
- Heady
- High-minded
- Lovers of pleasures more than lovers of God
- Having a form of godliness but denying the power thereof: from such turn away.
- For of this sort are they which creep into houses, and lead captive silly women laden with sins, led away with various lusts.
- Ever learning, and never able to come to the knowledge of the truth."

Coming out of COVID-19, people were speaking heartily about getting back to normal. Prior to the epidemic most church involvement was in person. Research shows that today only about 50% of adults are in attendance. 1 in 5 or 20% are still attending online. 1 in 4 (26%) is mixing online and in person worship. Additionally, we are finding an increasingly greater degree of decay of decency, morality, and frequency in threatening and vilifying any Christian candidate in an attempt to keep him or her from not only holding public office – but *make or show no public expression of their Christian beliefs and practices.* Again, we are reminded that *it is* the church *not* government, that is responsible for having a positive *moral influence on culture – and restraining evil.*

I repeat when we put our trust in secular leaders who are sympathetic to Christian beliefs – we tend to relax, back off, and let them drive. In many cases, local churches have actually abdicated their role in upholding a positive moral climate in their areas of influence. God forbid!

How much do I owe?

According to prophecy, namely Daniel 2, 7, and Revelation 13 and 17, a world leader and government are coming that will be both totalitarian and dictatorial. In the meantime, we will continue as government expands its reach into our lives, disrupting and hindering our freedoms. While conscious persecution of Christians will eventually become the daily norm here in America – as we continue the slide downhill toward Revelation 6.

As Jesus' disciples, we are *called* and *equipped* to live peaceful, respectful, and honorable lives in whatever culture and under the Government we find ourselves. (see Romans 12:18; 1 Peter 2:17). Yet there may come a time when, because of conscience and commitment to God and his Word, civil disobedience is necessary, leading us to stand when those all around us are bowing:

- All pastors are apologists. This means we *speak up for biblical truth* – when others are silent.
- It means *we act with integrity* when others are stuck in mediocracy, complacency, and deception.
- There will come a tragic and diabolical disintegration of the relationship between the government and the people.

As governments around the world intrude in their citizens' lives and infringe on their rights, we believers *must be discerning, recognizing the spirit of the age and the hope of deliverance is near.* And like those first-century apostolic believers, we must buildup love, and encourage *one another* as we *"see the day drawing near"* (Hebrews 10:25), thoroughly, unmoved by the deceiving winds of an evil culture and government.

**Remember governments are not divine,
but they are divinely appointed!**

No matter how good or effective human government is it still has *absolutely* no significant bearing on God's eternal kingdom. Don't be misled, it truly doesn't matter who is president or Caesar!

Christianity had its beginning and flourished, under one of the most godless, pagan governments the world has ever seen.

According to the prophet Isaiah, ultimately, politics, and presidents are irrelevant in the great plan of God's prophetic program:

> *"He brings the princes to nothing;*
> *He makes the judges of the earth*
> *Useless.*
> *Scarcely shall they be planted.*
> *Scarcely shall they be sown.*
> *Scarcely shall their stock take root in*
> *The earth,*
> *When He will also blow on them,*
> *And they will wither,*
> *And the whirlwind will take them*
> *Away like stubble;*
> *"To whom then will you liken Me,*
> *Or in whom shall I be equal?" says*
> *The Holy One.* Isaiah 40:23-25

Nothing and useless" expresses the insignificance of entire nations before the might of the Living God. *"To whom will you liken Me?"* Notice the same imagery in v. 17, describing God's judgment. This and the following in v. 18, form part of an important biblical theme, the incomparability of God (see v. 25). Satan knows what time it is! So, moving forward, we should anticipate an increasingly greater moral decay, and basically in the area of politics.

One big problem, we find ourselves defending is the non-biblical (ideal TV nuclear family model of the 1950s/ and 60s). The family is eroding, but the problem is that we find ourselves as stated above defending a non-biblical idea. Striving to maintain this tradition, has been disastrous from an evangelistic perspective. Our Christian families and homes should and must be places of peace, where the Church is viewed as Jesus' community of the redeemed from all walks of life. Praise God for Jesus' "whosoever."

THE MARRIAGE SUPPER OF THE LAMB

In Revelation 19:6-9, John said, *"I heard as it were, the voice of a great multitude, as the sound of many waters and as the sound of mighty thundering, saying, "Alleluia! For the Lord God Omnipotent reigns!" Let us be glad and rejoice and give Him glory, for the marriage supper of the Lamb has come, and the wife has made herself ready." And to her it was granted to be arrayed in fine linen, clean and bright, for the fine linen <u>is the righteous acts of the saints</u>. Then he said to me, "Write: Blessed are those who are called to the marriage supper of the Lamb!" KJV*

Then I, John, saw the holy city, New Jerusalem, coming down out of heaven from God, prepared, as a bride adorned for her husband. And I heard a loud voice from heaven saying, "Behold the tabernacle of God is with men, and He will dwell with them, and they shall be His people. God Himself will be with them and be their God." (Revelation 21:2-3 NKJV)

In so many cases our *fears* restrict us from letting go of control and safety we have spent years cultivating. This culture of fear is totally inconsistent with Jesus' redemption vision of the kingdom of God. Sadly, our churches and church leaders are not challenging us to move beyond this crisis. The nuclear family model is not adequate for the church.

So, we are talking about the family of God here where Jesus Himself defines it. The idolized nuclear family (as perceived in many churches) is not the primary means of God's grace and salvation for a waiting and desperate world. Rather the church is God's agent commissioned to fulfill these functions. We will have further discussion on the family in chapter 7.

Restoring or refocusing the family of God does not begin with the nation or with the family itself. It begins with the Church.[17] The model family then, is a warm inviting environment where people can get a glimpse of true community, and therefore of heaven. Amen!

---

[17]   Rodney Clapp, *Families at the Crossroads: Beyond Traditional and Modern Options* (Downers Grove, IL: Inter Varsity Press, 1993).

STUDY GUIDE: WORKSHEET AND REFLECTIONS
CHAPTER 5

1. Human parents are still God's first _____.

2. The first place our Christian faith should go to _____ is in the _____, where the kingdom of God is the first priority.

3. The _____ _____ that is seen, practiced, and modeled in the home usually has a greater impact and influence than any other place.

4. We have the daily responsibility of devoting ourselves more and more to God so that in spirit, soul, and body, we completely belong to Him.

5. Our worldview determines our view for the world. Our worldview _____ our values, and our values _____ our behavior.

6. To the _____ view there is no such thing as absolute truth. Absolute truth does exist.

7. Morality has been _____ opposing personal or social convictions.

8. The "Big Lie" is, I don't _____ _____.

9. Restoring or refocusing the model family of God begins with the _____.

Chapter Six

A CHANGED MINDSET

"Train up a child in the way he should go; even when he is old, he will not depart from it." (Proverbs 22:6 ESV)

In his autobiography *Just as I Am,* Evangelist Billy Graham recalled an unforgettable conversation he had with President John F. Kennedy shortly after his election. On the way back to the Kennedy house, the president-elect stopped the car and turned to me. "Do you believe in the Second Coming of Jesus Christ?" He asked.

"I must certainly do"

"Well, does my church believe it?" Kennedy inquired.

"They have it in creeds, "I replied.

"They don't preach it," he said. "They don't tell us much about it. I'd like to know what you think."

I explained what the Bible said about Christ coming the first time, dying on the cross, rising from the dead, and then promising he would come back again. "Only then, "I said, "are we going to have permanent world peace."

"Very interesting," he said looking away. "We'll have to talk more about that someday."[18] And he drove on.

---

[18]   Billy Graham, *Just As I Am* is published by Harper Collins Worldwide (Harper Collins and Zondervan, 1997/2007) 395.

Several years later, the two met again, this time at the 1963 National Prayer Breakfast. Graham wrote:

I had the flu. After I gave my short talk, and he gave his, we walked out of the hotel to his car together, as was always our custom. At the curb he returned to me.

"Billy, could you ride back to the White House with me? I'd like to see you for a minute."

"Mr. President, I've got a fever." I protested. "Not only am I weak, but I don't want to give you this thing. Couldn't we wait and talk some other time?"[19]

It was a cold, snowy day, and I was freezing as I stood there without my overcoat. "Of course," he said graciously.

Sadly, the preacher and the president would never meet again. Later that year. President Kennedy was assassinated in Dallas, Texas. Dr. Graham comments, "His hesitation at the car door, and his request, haunts me still. What was on his mind? Should I have gone with him? It was an irrecoverable moment.[20]

An irrecoverable moment. And a missed opportunity.

Dr. Graham's encounter with President Kennedy demonstrates a life principle and spiritual law. Each such encounter for each of us can be like doors of opportunity. If we can identify with this as a personal teachable moment, an open door, or if not careful a fleeting opportunity? We can capture the opportunity, or it can be lost. We have the opportunity with Gen Y's and Zers, knowing that God's judgment is drawing closer with each passing day. We better get in a hurry!

This principle was pursued in Noah's life. God opened the door for Noah with a mission, "[build an ark]" a 120-year God-given project for him. During that entire period, Noah preached God's truth of righteousness to his generation. We are not told the specific words, of Noah, but we can certainly, assume that like Billy Graham for so many faithful years kept his gospel preaching focused and on point.

---

[19]   Ibid. pg. 397
[20]   "Billy Graham" Just As I Am (Pg. 399).

75

A Culture of Evangelism

If you are a part of a healthy church, then it should have a healthy culture of evangelism. We are concerned with a deeply spiritual and biblical concept. Jesus laid down this concept with two essential commands for an effective evangelism culture in the healthy church. He said, "By this all people will know that you are My disciples, if you love one another."(John 13:35 ESV)

Later on, during the same session with His disciples, He prayed that they would be unified, "that the world may know that You sent Me ..." (John 17:20-21 NKJV) According to Jesus, Himself, our love for one another in the church is a statement, that we are truly born again from above. And when we are unified in the church, we show to the world that Jesus is the Son of God. 1) Love confirms discipleship. 2) Unity confirms Christ's deity.

Digital Evangelism

In the case of digital evangelism, all rules have changed just as other topics discussed in this book. Especially since the COVID epidemic, the church has a mission field that looks different than all others in the past. The digital field is every tongue and ethnic group the world over. As we've explained in other areas of evangelism, this mission field requires everyone working in unity to reach it for the glory of God.

A couple of decades ago, no one could fantom the apps and websites we used to post pictures of individual or family travel, and display food we have eaten would become the same mode – to see souls saved and disciples sent into all the world. Who would have dreamed that You Tube, Instagram, Facebook, and Tik Tok would ever be used to convey the gospel to the world. My interest in digital ministry began one day when my great grandson, Jaytonio observed my audience and operation, and after a little snicker told me how digital ministry would open doors to his Gen Z'ers.

THE LOCAL CHURCH IS THE GOSPEL MADE VISIBLE

As we picture the gospel in our love for one another – it needs to be done in a local congregation of people covenanted together in love to be a church. Many think that Christians are strange, yet they are continuously drawn into the fellowship by the love among the members. The gospel is pictured also in the many biblical instructions God has weaved into the very fabric of the church that, when properly done, serves as proclamations of the gospel.

Too often we forget that Jesus is building His church so while pursuing a healthy culture of evangelism, we don't remake His church for evangelism. Instead, through the guidance and power of the Holy Spirit, we allow those things that God built into church to proclaim the gospel.

Jesus did not forget the gospel when He built His church. For example:

- Baptism pictures the death, burial, and resurrection of Jesus.
- The Lord's Supper proclaims the death and resurrection of Christ until He returns and prompts us to confess our sins and experience forgiveness anew.
- In our prayers, we pray the truths of God's Word.
- We sing praises of the great things God has done for us through the gospel.
- We give financially to advance the gospel message.
- The preaching and teaching of the Word brings the gospel.

The Word of God preached, forms the church, once formed the church is given the task of making disciples, who are sent to preach the gospel to form new churches. This process has been taking place since Jesus ascended into heaven and will continue until He returns for His Church.

THE BREAD OF LIFE

Many churches frown on people who have recognized they have the call and responsibility to reach out to people with the gospel. They minister when and wherever the opportunity presents itself. Then there are those who believe that reaching out is the responsibility of the church only.

Since a culture of evangelism is grassroots, rather than hierarchal, every healthy church understands and has a culture of evangelism as witnessed in their principles and practices. Certainly, the church supports and prays for outreach and evangelistic opportunities – but the church's role is not to run programs. The church should cultivate *a culture of evangelism*. The *members* (all) are *equipped* and sent out from the church to do evangelism. This is right!

DO WE REALLY UNDERSTAND THE CHURCH?

Through training in the military, we learned that a couple of degrees off with a azimuth or while reading a map (Vietnam) could actually land you in the enemy's camp. In some areas of the world a couple of degrees off could land you across the border and into another country. It's true! On the battlefield in Ukraine today – it is reported that the Russian pilots have operated and bombed targets just a few feet from the border of Poland and other nearby countries. Well here before the 1st year of war has ended, the obvious has happened – a weapon of war from some part of the battlefield has exploded across the border in Poland.

A check of a map or globe easily confirms the big problems that can result from a small course deviation or error in the case today it could trigger (World War III). And the same is true in the church. The problem with people in paragraph 1 above, in reference to evangelism is not their view of evangelism, but it is with not understanding the church. Understanding the church helps us get the right GPS heading for evangelism.

One of our great joys when my wife and I were planting the Bread of Life Ministries, was flying by faith; seeing the hand of God work. Think about it, you are at AAA getting your oil changed and someone walked up with a pen and clipboard in hand and asked, "Please define "church" for me. Can you answer? Then he follows up with, "What are the necessary components of a church?" Does that question stump you?

If so, you are not alone. Magdalene and I were blessed to actually live with and visit missionaries in Central and South America (3 years – and 2 years in the Republic of South Korea) while serving 26.5 years in the U.S. Army before retirement July 1, 1984. Many of these people call themselves church planters. They are wonderful people.

Nowhere did we find structured programs for outreach, but rather for you to think how *you* can reach out. I would suggest you learn something about the culture, and about their struggles. Reach out and invite the friends you make to come with you to your homes, and you go to theirs, small group Bible study or church – with the purpose of commending the gospel among them. It's not just about being friendly, though that needs to happen – but there need to be an awareness that we are in this together.

SLEEPWALKING TO THE RAPTURE

In spite of our ill behavior as a nation, God has truly blessed America through Christianity. Somehow through slavery, wars, racism, misguided ideologies and many other obstacles wrought by Satan and mankind – I believe the outcome thus far was preordained and the whole world has been blessed as a result.

However, many nations throughout history have been used of God for His purposes and later, they lose His favor. The Scripture says, "The wicked shall be turned into hell, and all the nations that forget God." (Psalm 9:17)

In their book *"Black Eye for America,* Carol M. Swain PhD, and Christopher J. Schorr PhD listed four important aspects in which Christianity helped shape the United States:

- The most obvious is the direct influence of Christianity and of its antecedent, Judaism had on American culture through the faith traditions of the American people.
- The second distinct source of Christian influence the "civil religion." The institutionalized, national *public* faith, which is distinct from Christianity, and the other *private* religions of the American people.
- America's decentralization and limited system of government reflects the framers' view, that religion would supplement state power in preserving social order. At the beginning nearly every American was a Christian, so religion meant Christianity – later the framer's view changed to say that *any* religious belief can carry the weight of private and public morality in a free society.
- Christianity provided the guard rails around the liberal political tradition; it also shaped the development of that tradition.

Realize that at that time nearly every American was a Christian.[21] The West's *secular liberal inheritance* also owes much to its Christian religious inheritance. Taken together, the influence of Christian thinking on classically liberal and conservative values is profound.[22] The American colonies were basically Christians. *Religious freedom* was the prime mover at that time and should be today in every Christian community. Like everything else, if we get careless and forget to counter the ills facing us daily as they appear from every corner – we could lose it.

Prayerfully, no one is breathing down your neck about hindering or stopping your daily prayers or Bible reading from your own personal Bible. Were we shaken to the core from the very thought that government controlled the shutdown of churches across America – but not the abortion apparatus; which continued operations throughout that whole period?

---

[21] Carol M. Swain PhD and Christopher J. Schorr PhD, *Black Eye for America* (Logos Books 2021) 39

[22] 8 Ibid. 41

Thus, Christianity helped shape the nation's laws, holidays, and customs. Research shows that prominent universities were founded with the goal of teaching the Christian faith and promoting Christian understanding of public virtue. That was the case during that period. What about today? How will this nation boast the nearly 100% Christian at its founding which was slightly reduced in every generation, however the downward spiral has increased in speed that during this present 21st century to less than 40% Christians?

A New Creation

The time of the Gentiles has now been around 2000 years. What we are not coming into is another time of the Jews as was the case of their own 2000 years of time of the Jews. But today God is bringing about a time of the "born again from above Jew" and "the born again from above" Gentile grafted into one *new* creation in Christ – His body, the Church. This new entity is "the spiritual seed" of Abraham. The Scripture says, "For you are all sons of God through faith in Christ Jesus. For as many of you baptized into Christ have put on Christ. There is neither Jew nor Greek, there is neither slave nor free, there is neither male nor female; for you are all one in Christ Jesus. And if you are Christ's, then you are Abraham's seed, and heirs according to promise." (Galatians 3:26-29 NKJV)

This passage of Scripture should put to rest the so-called "replacement theology" embraced by many in the church today. That is, the belief that all of the present purposes for Israel will be replaced by the church. Certainly, this belief has clouded the truth for some time, but the truth of the matter is clear in the Book of Romans where the apostle Paul clearly established God's purpose for each. He also warned against becoming, **"arrogant toward the natural branches"** (see Romans 11:18) and **"Do not be conceited, but fear; for if God did not spare the natural branches, neither will He spare you."** (see Romans 11:20b-21) God has not rejected (Natural Israel forever)!

THE DISTORTION OF REALITY

As I stated in an earlier section, the devil uses people, governments, and social media as primary tools to sow deception and division between people. Although this may not be the intention – it is certainly the effect. In these postmodern times the news itself is a gross *distortion of reality*. Only the most extreme events make the news, and most of them are acts of violence and malicious destruction. Good news does not sell – but even the good that makes the news is not a *true* perception of reality. News of domestic violence is never balanced by news of the many happy families around us. The news itself presents a very distorted and dismal picture of life in America.

Even the Christian media, when striving to do an honest job of reporting interesting events at church, often creates an unreal perception of Christianity for their own Christian readers. While the average church in America is not like the churches that are newsworthy, but average churches in their specific communities are probably doing for more to accomplish a true advancement for the gospel. These average churches are also a more accurate reflection of the true state of Christianity today, good, or bad. Even when the intention is not to distort, the very nature of the postmodern media does *distort reality.*

PULLING DOWN STRONGHOLDS

Strongholds are lies that people believe. The more people who believe a lie, the more powerful that stronghold will be. The enemy is using the media to sow a demented perception of almost everything. When the average family compares their lives to those of the television family, they often come away disappointed with what they have – and who they are. The overall effect of this is to blur reality. I could go on and on – but the bottom line to the Christian is, *only the church*, has been given the Spirit of Truth, and the grace and power required to pull down these strongholds of misconceptions, and false judgments. The divinely powerful weapons that God has given to us are designed to tear down strongholds (see 2 Corinthians 10:3-5). It is imperative that we use them! God's plan for our lives, is to *conform us in character and power to the image of Jesus Christ.* If we fail to see our relationship to God as such, we will allow areas within us to remain unchanged.

Pulling down strongholds is the demolition and removal of these old ways of thinking so that the Presence of Jesus Christ can be manifested through us.

All successful *deliverance* must begin by first removing that which defends the enemy. Paul in speaking of *spiritual warfare* injects the word "stronghold" (KJV) to define the *spiritual fortresses* wherein Satan and his demons hide and are protected. These fortresses exist in the *thought patterns* and *ideas* that govern individuals and churches, as well as communities, cities, and nations. Before victory is claimed, these strongholds must be pulled down and Satan's armor removed. Then the mighty weapons of the Word of God and the Spirit working in tandem can effectively empty Satan's house.

A stronghold can be a source of protection for us *from* the devil, as is the case when the Lord becomes our stronghold (see Psalm 18:2). Or a stronghold can be a source of defense for the devil – where *demonic* or *sinful activity* is actually *defended* within us by our sympathetic thoughts toward evil:

- I think this has been the case with many *sympathetic* pastors and congregations that defend and protect people's *openly* sinful lifestyles; which are plainly condemned through God's Word.
- The strongholds we are going to expose first are wrong attitudes that *protect the old self-life.* These strongholds often become "fortified dwellings" of demonic oppression in a person's life.

Your rebellion toward God provides a
place for the devil in your life.

As we saw earlier, Lucifer's five "I wills" in (see Isaiah 14:13-14). God had no choice but to judge Lucifer. God cast him from heaven down to earth (Ezekiel 28:16), exiling him from the heavenly government and his place of authority (see Luke 10:18). At that time his name was changed from Lucifer ("morning star) to Satan ("adversary"). Just as Satan fell through *pride*, so he seeks for Christians to fall through pride. In Scripture we see many examples of Satan's tempting through pride:

- Part of Satan's temptation of Eve was, "You will be like God" (see Genesis 3:5).
- Part of Satan's influence on David to take a consensus of fighting men in Israel related to David's pride at the strength of his forces.
- Some even tried to tempt Jesus through human pride: "The devil took Him to a very high mountain and showed Him all the kingdoms of the world and their glory. And he said to Him, "All these things I will give You if You will fall down and worship me." (Matthew 4:8-9 NKJV)

Scripture understandably warns that "a church leader must not be a new believer,[23] because he might become proud, and the devil would cause him to fall" (1 Timothy 3:6 NLT). It is no wonder that Peter speaks of the need for humility in the same context as speaking about the devil:

Therefore, "humble yourselves under the mighty hand of God, that He may exalt you in due time, casting all your cares upon Him, for He cares for you. Be sober, be vigilant; because your adversary the devil walks about like a roaring lion, seeking whom he may devour." (1 Peter 5:6-8 NKJV)

We should present all our worries, anxieties, and problems to God in order to let Him handle them. Peter warns us to be self-disciplined, dispense with foolish thinking. Be alert to the spiritual pitfalls of life and take appropriate steps to make certain that we do

---

[23] "novice" in the KJV.

not stumble. Who better than Peter would know about the prowling of Satan.

Finally, in these last days the *worship of success* is normally the form of "idol worship" the devil cultivates in us through pride. Under the influences of success today, Christians have stopped asking in whose name and at what price did I pay to achieve … many have cast down the cross of Christ. They are intoxicated with success! Even some Black Churches stand with pride but will not bow in humility. At what price are we willing to take the cross in to the world *and identify with our Savior?*

There is a new phenomenon in the church – we have seen the gospel neglected and even mocked by some religious liberals, conservatives, and nominal Christians that is to be expected.

We must always remember – God is neither
Democrat nor Republican!

We must always remember that God is neither Republican nor Democrat. What is different today is the gospel message of the cross is being ignored even by those who claim to be saved by its message. Today it is crucial that the gospel be proclaimed most clearly, but we are hearing muffled voices even from some of the greatest pulpits in this country. In many denominations psychology is substituted for theology. Science is substituted for truth and self is seen as a god today. In short, we have lost our intellectual and spiritual center.

BE HUMBLE

Likewise you younger people, submit yourselves to your elders. Yes, all of you be submissive to one another, and be clothed with humility, for God resists the proud, but gives grace to the humble. (1 Peter 5:5 NKJV)

I believe verse 5 is literally to the young people of the church, but we may apply it to all members as they follow their spiritual leaders (see Hebrews 13:17). Here, Peter is referring to the evening in the Upper Room when Jesus washed the disciples feet. To be *"clothed with humility."* It means to be controlled by a humble spirit, to be a servant. God resists arrogant, self-seeking persons but gives grace to the humble. (Proverbs 3:34; James 4:6)

STUDY GUIDE: WORKSHEET AND REFLECTIONS
CHAPTER 6

1. If you are part of a healthy church, then it should have a healthy _____ of _____.

2. Love confirms _____ and _____ confirms deity.

3. Christians are drawn into the fellowship by the _____ among the _____.

4. The Word of God preached, forms the church, once formed the church is given the _____ of _____ _____.

5. This passage of Scripture (Galatians 3:26-29) should put to rest the so-called "_____ _____ _____."

6. Strongholds are _____ that people believe.

7. The Christian is the only one given _____ of Truth.

Section Two

UPON THIS ROCK

Chapter Seven

REFOCUSING THE FAMILY

"So that through the church the manifold wisdom of God might now be made known to the rulers and authorities in heavenly places." (Ephesians 3:10 ESV)

In this chapter, we are primarily concerned with the way in which we refocus and live out what it means to be the family of God. "Every believer is a church planter; and every church is a church-planting church" is one of the most powerful mantras ever. It's a great slogan, not simply because it is the key to unlocking the post COVID-19 church, but because it recaptures a major tenet of that which was hidden of the Reformation Movement, "the priesthood of all believers" at the same time communicating the potential that is contained in every individual disciple. It establishes the fact that every believer is a priest of Jesus Christ, our High Priest. Therefore, he or she has within them the potential for transforming the world. I came across this old illustration in my files: A teacher held out his hand which held an acorn, he had three boys to come up front. He asked each of the three what they saw in his hand. The first said, "I see an acorn." The second said, I see and oak tree." The third exclaimed, "I see a whole forest of oak trees."

In these few statements we see the great potential power of the church of Jesus Christ with the Holy Spirit inside of us (individually and corporately). As a seed contains the full potential of the tree, so the tree contains the full potential of the forest. However, it's all there in the seed in the first place. Again, recognizing the world-transforming power of the gospel and God's people are absolutely essential to becoming an apostolic New Testament Church again.

THE ROLE OF THE HOLY SPIRIT

Jesus promised the disciples in the Upper Room, "I will ask the Father, and He will give you another Helper, to be with you forever, even the Spirit of truth …" (John 14:16:17 ESV) The word *helper* carries the meaning of "counselor, comforter, advocate, one who strengthens." These concepts of encouragement, support, care, the shouldering of responsibility for another's welfare, and advocating truth are all conveyed of by this one word (helper). The Holy Spirit's relevance in the church cannot be overstated. Two Greek terms translate into the word *another.* The first means *"another of a different kind."* The second means *"another of the same kind."* John 14:16 uses the second word. Jesus said He would ask the Father to send another Helper *of the same kind* as Himself. That is, a personal, ever-present helper. This next statement is vitally important! In fact, our survival in life depends on it. Just as Jesus was a personal comforter who helped the disciples for three years during His earthly ministry – so also would followers of Christ (believers) have another personal comforter, the Holy Spirit, who would not just be with them but in them throughout their lives. Sadly, many think of the Book of Acts merely as a history of the beginning of the church. The church is the body of Christ and the last words He spoke to His body (disciples), at His ascension, were:

"But you will receive power when the Holy Spirit has come upon you, and you will be my witnesses in Jerusalem and in all Judea and Samaria, and to the ends of the earth." (Acts 1:8 ESV)

Christ has continued to speak to His body, the church, continuously for the past 2000 years from His throne in heaven by the Holy Spirit as promised. The Book of Acts is the only book in the

Bible without an ending, it is still being written concerning the Acts of His body, the church (His present-day disciples).

SPIRITUAL FORMATION

To incorporate all, spiritual formation begins best in the home. Actually, a strong Christian family is God's design for the world. God wants every family to be under His authority, under His care and protection, secure in His love. Day by day, the home is to be a place of safety; where the living faith is seen, practiced, and then modeled, with greater impact and influence than any other location. The two places of most joy should be the home and church. The work of the church is powerfully important – to continue and reinforce what effective spiritual outcomes that godly parenting has accomplished in the home. These godly outcomes are so important in development of a strong spiritual foundation. The Bible has a much larger vision of the family unit, going well beyond the nuclear model to include grandparents, friends, and the stranger. Therefore, they provide the greatest potential for a lifelong spiritual impact and maturity.

The local church must refocus on their children and young adults because Jesus did! He was very clear about the importance of children. He blessed them, laid hands on them, prayed for them and made it clear that, "unless you turn and become like little children, you will never enter the kingdom of heaven." "Whoever humbles himself like this child is the greatest in the kingdom of heaven." (Matthew 18:3, 4 ESV) Jesus also explicitly warned about causing children to sin (prayerfully study Matthew 18 and 19).

One of the consequences of the injustice and evils of racial discrimination in this country today has done grievous damage to the identity and self-esteem of our children. This trauma has lifelong consequences.

Let The Little Children Come

There is a record in the Bible when Jesus' disciples wanted to keep children away from Him so that He could attend to more important things. He rebuked them by telling them *not* to take the children away, for all of us *need* to learn from their kind of faith (see Matthew 19:13-15).

He is telling us that we need the children and can learn from them, not the other way around. All of our children will tell you that they loved being a part of the worship services with Magdalene and me. As I explained in an earlier section, this has been the way for our family to the fourth generation.

Integrating children into every aspect of a church community is not just good for the kids; it's also beneficial to adults in ways you can't imagine. We are living in a time when families are falling apart or replaced with cohabitation. Parenthood is God's idea, and so is marriage. Tragically, both are almost lost vocations today. With all succeeding generations things get worse. Why is this happening?

- Dysfunctional parents pass on their flaws to the next generation.
- The flaws are added on to before being passed on to the grandchildren.
- This snowball effect of dysfunction is gaining speed as it races downhill.
- This downhill move of dysfunction is destroying many lives and increasingly our whole society is dissolving (wasting away).

Part of the reason for this most desperate situation is that it is more challenging than ever to find an appropriate model of parenting. In the church we have programs, seminars, and books to help teach about parenting:

- But few good examples in church.
- New parents cannot actually watch a seasoned parent respond to his or her children and teach by example.

- The church has parents who do not know how to train their children.
- Some see children as an interruption.
- In too many families the father is missing.
- People forget the evil forces who are determined to destroy the family.

Child Abuse

One of the most severe warnings ever issued in all of history was issued by the Lord Jesus to adults who abuse children:

"And *whosoever shall offend one of these little ones that believe in me, it is better for him that a millstone were hanged about his neck, and he were cast into the sea. And if thy hand offend thee [by abusing a child], cut it off: it is better for thee to enter into life maimed, than having two hands to go to hell, into the fire that never shall be quenched: where their worm dieth not, and the fire is not quenched. And if thy foot offend thee [by abusing a child], cut it off: it is better for thee to enter halt into life, than having two feet to be cast into hell, into the fire that never shall be quenched: where their worm dieth not, and the fire is not quenched. And if thine eye offend thee [by lusting after a child], pluck it out: it is better for thee to enter the kingdom of God with one eye, than having two eyes to be cast into hell fire: where their worm dieth not, and the fire is not quenched.*" (Mark 9:42-48 KJV) Brackets are mine.

INCLUDE GEN ZERS

If we would think of the community of faith as a family rather than a weekly religious event, then you will see differently the whole reality of what it should be. Children are family; therefore, they do not interrupt. Family learns from one another – and that includes other parents. In the local church, young parents who were raised with poor role models can learn how to parent children well. This is difficult if we continue to separate the family according to age-appropriate groupings – in all of church life.

It takes a lot of courage for a young couple to admit they don't know how to properly raise their children – but they probably won't ask for help, unless they have actually seen parents who appear to know what they are doing. Of course, we need to teach each other, but the best form of learning involves putting the lesson into practice. It is also true that the children often teach the adults.

If we are to view church as a spiritual family, we must include Gen Zers in the mix. It is imperative that we allow our children to carry some of the responsibility of church life, then they will learn and share in the church experience. Our churches will be better, both now and in the future as the Gen Zers grow up and take on leadership as adults. It is so sad that we go to church religiously and leave our children home to roam the streets. No wonder, the following statistics show up among pollsters:

- 1 in 4 respondents aged 13-24 (Gen Zers) said they have very little tolerance for people with beliefs I don't agree with.
- Almost 1 in 2 Gen Zers agreed with the statement that, "some people deserved to be cancelled," while just a 3rd of over 25's expressed the same opinion.
- Less than half held the view that there are "only two genders" compared with 68% of their elders.

A closer look at Gen Zers

Although some Gen Zers are hungry for God and fearless in their faith, the reality is that the majority are disconnected from church. According to a significant study conducted earlier this year (2022) by the Survey Center on American Life of the *American Enterprise Institute*, Gen Z is the least religious generation, and the most fatherless generation ever. More than one-third (34%) are "religiously unaffiliated," compared to 29% of Millennials, 25% Gen Xers, 18% of Baby Boomers, and 9% of the Silent Generation. Further 9% of Gen Zers identify as atheist and 9% as agnostic. Other significant trends:

- Of those Gen Zers who are religiously unaffiliated, 43% said they grew up in a nonreligious home.

- 39% of Gen Zers said they feel lonely at least once a week.
- Only 40% of Gen Zers agree that raising children in a religious tradition is important.
- Among 18-29-year-olds, 74% said they were 17 or younger when they no longer identified with the religion they grew up with.
- In 2021, 37% of the public reported having confidence in religious institutions, a major decline since 2001 when 60% reported feeling confidence.
- Gen Zers is the largest generation in American history, representing 27% of the population (Asian 6%, Black 14%, Hispanic 25%, Caucasian 52%).
- 22% has at least one immigrant parent.
- Gen Zers are on track to be the most well-educated generation yet.
- They are tech-savvy, with little or no memory of life without smartphones as the average Gen Zers got their first smartphone just before their 12 birthdays.
- They spend an average of 2 hours and 55 minutes on social media a day.
- The majority prefer streaming services to traditional cable.
- Only 13% live in rural America.
- 40% of 19-year-old Gen Zers in America don't have a driver's license.
- They are pro-government; 70% believe that the government should do more to solve problems.[24]

Damaging dysfunctions

A through refocusing here is likely to open us up to significant new possibilities and new models and new ways in which to live out our walk with Jesus. If how we think generations Y and Z profoundly affects the nature of discipleship, then the same is true for the church.

---

[24] Accessed 11/22/22https//businessinsider.com/gen-z-most-accomplished-loneliest-blame-parentsfaultforit2022-4 American Enterprise Institute.

There are distorted views and perspectives as to what the great number of local churches think and are doing about the absence of children, youth, and younger adults in all of our churches. Certainly, such dysfunctions damage our witness and our capacity to live out the gospel message.

When we see ourselves in the light of the biblical narrative, forsaking false cultural definitions, and the traditions of men, we can see the redemptive impulse of God reaching out through His people into a lost and broken generation.

Through, faithful disciples of Jesus like yourselves gathered in churches, the extraordinary plan of God (salvation for all who will receive it), is becoming known and talked about even among the angels (see Eph. 3:10).

OTHER CHALLENGES [FOR ALL]

Any serious discussion of American values and traditions must therefore address the role of Christianity in the American Creed. Let me say up front, non-Christian Americans are not in any sense, less authentically American; my aim rather is to be true to the context in which American values and principles developed.

The influence of Christian thinking on liberal and conservative values is profound. Christianity has helped shape this nation through the faith traditions of the American people. From childhood we've heard that this nation is, or at least once was a Christian nation.

It has been argued that this is an inaccurate notion by many people. Their reason being that Christian means "Christlike," and a check of history would prove that this nation has never acted Christlike. We have argued that it is impossible for any version of the kingdom of this world to be Christlike and neither can it be said that it even acts like Christ.

However, as stated earlier the faith traditions of the American people have certainly helped to shape America.

The kingdom of God, which *always* looks like Jesus, can never be considered an improved version of the kingdom of this world. To get around this, a *counterfeit Christianity* has been *superimposed* and *substituted* in the place of true Christianity when and where needed. When a church gets caught up in cultural trends, no matter whether left or right, more than likely it will miss the heart of the gospel.

When that happens, the unity found in Christ is broken, and too often the gospel is omitted from the picture, compromised, or misconstrued. As stated earlier, there is a nationalistic deistic civil religion weaved into this country that has many believing it is authentic Christianity. Even though America is largely secularized today this Christianization is often used secularly; for example, the Christianization of a military force was used by President George W. Bush as he depicted America as being on a holy "crusade" against "evildoers." On another occasion, he said that America is the "light of the world," which the "darkness" (that is, our national enemies) could not extinguish.[25]

As is typical with civil religions, if questioned on the impact these people's faith has on their lives, the answer would be nil to none. Barna research shows that the majority of professing Christians lack even a basic understanding of the faith they profess.

On that same line, Critical Race Theory (CRT) has proven itself to be more than indirectly opposed to true Christianity. Owen Strachan, in his book, *Christianity and Wokeness*,[26] reads, the opposite group of people as irreversibly innocent. One group is always the villain, the other group is always the victim. We are told that victims (defined by the color of their skin) have nothing to repent because they are not in power; therefore, they cannot be racist. But their oppressors (also defined by the color of their skin) are forever guilty.

The distinction made by Dr. Ibram X. Kendi between, in his words, "liberation" and "savior" theologies, describes "liberation" as

---

[25]   See the PBS *Frontline* special, "The Jesus Factor." See George W. Bush, "Advancing the Cause of Freedom," speech delivered April 17, 2001.

[26]   Owen Strachan, *Christianity and Wokeness, How the Social Justice Movement Is Hijacking the Gospel – and the Way to Stop It* (Washington, DC: Salem Books, 2021), 109.

a commitment to radical social activism, through a vision of Jesus Christ as a political revolutionary struggling against oppression.

He then describes the "savior" theology where individual sinners are saved through their faith in Jesus Christ. Christians and non-Christians alike recognize Christianity in "savior theology." However, Kendi goes on to say that "antiracists" CRT advocates, must *reject* savior theology (Christianity Because):

> It ... goes right in line with racist ideals and racist theology in which they say, you know what, black people ... other racial groups, the reason why they're struggling on earth is because what they are behaviorally doing wrong and it is my job as the pastor to sort of save these wayward black people or wayward poor people or wayward queer people. This type of theology breeds bigotry.[27]

Dr. Kenda's claims here are consistent with his earlier referenced claims regarding the meaning of racial disparities. For example, "sin" is to be found in oppressive power structures, not in individual people. It certainly doesn't reside in the victims of oppression.[28]

AMERICAN NATIONALISM

As I ponder today's definition of American Nationalism[29], it's quite apparent that there are many interpretations of what it really is. From a community that includes ethnical, racial, and cultural,

---

[27] Woke Preacher Clips, Ibram Kendi: *Antichrists Fundamentally Reject "Savior Theology"* [video], You Tube, 2021, https//www.youtube.com/watch?v=azJh4n69Q5k&tql61s

[28] Ibid.

[29] American Nationalism is a form of civic, ethnical, cultural, or economic influences found in the United States. Eventually, it indicates the aspects that distinguishes the U.S as an autonomous political community. cultural nationalism follows along with America nationalism. It forms group allegiances based on common cultural heritage rather than race or political party. Also included are language, Christianity, history, national symbols. This concept fuses cultural nationalism and religion. Accessed 8/29/22, at https//en.wikipedia.org/wiki/American Nationalism.

called civic nationalism as an autonomous liberal community. Then we have the conservative arm that forms allegiance based on a common heritage rather than race or political party.

When American Nationalism favors the common heritage of the nation whether that only includes white conservatives and leaving out all others. Then all others *except* the African American still have a national flag. For many years I flew our American flag out in front of our home (before and after my retirement from the military).

Sadly, I removed it to my office for I do not want to offend anyone, since it has so many new interpretations and connotations of meaning. It has been made a symbol for extreme conservatism, fuel for the fires of a political party, symbol of an American heritage that all cannot share or feel a part of, for some the American flag has become their god, these are just a few observations. Other Americans no matter what their country of birth has their flag, even immigrants from Africa. What flag does the African American comfortably display?

I am proud to have served 26.5 years and retired a Command Sergeant Major from the U.S. Army, even volunteering to go and fight in Vietnam (1967/68). Always the proud American, loving God and country.

When people rage against God – they rebel against His truth!

THE GOSPEL TRUTH

I received my call into the gospel ministry while serving in the Republic of South Korea. I was proud to serve, as a Christian. I accepted Christ as my personal Savior as a teenager and entered the Army after graduating from high school. At that time (1958) religion was a part of our problem-solving process with appropriate guidance in TM 22-100, the U.S. Army Leadership Manual (at that time).

God was at the top of the Chain of Command, then. Christ was in my life the entire 26.5 years of service. Conviction of sins and repentance was always present with me. At times during that period,

I certainly didn't always look and act like a Christian, but I never gave up – but more important, neither did God! But long before my retirement in 1984, human secularism had put a big footprint on Christianity and the Chaplaincy in the Military. A heart for God was our strength then and still is today!

A counterfeit Christianity (spirit of Babylon) is parading along beside true Christianity today claiming to be the real thing. What mockery – it is with an anti-God theme (there is no requirement for the spiritual, we don't need God?). The counterfeit Christianity's god is called goodness. (i.e. thank goodness). Only the true Christianity can penetrate this satanic darkness. Sadly, we seem to have forgotten who we are and whose we are in Christ. "In Christ Jesus" you are all children of God through faith," Paul wrote to the Galatians. They had become so through the ritual of that embodies death and resurrection:

"Therefore, if anyone is in Christ, he is a new creation: old things have passed away; behold all things have become new."[30] "There is neither Jew nor Greek, there is neither slave nor free, there is neither male nor female, for you are all one in Christ Jesus. And if you are Christ's, then you are Abraham's seed, and heirs according to the promise."[31]

The results of being in Christ, one is *reconnected to God.* The way to life in Christ is by dying and rising with Christ:

"And all things are of God, who hath reconciled us unto Himself by Christ Jesus, and hath given to us the ministry of reconciliation; to wit that God was in Christ, reconciling the world unto Himself, not imputing their trespasses unto them; and hath committed unto us the word of reconciliation. Now then we are ambassadors for Christ, as though God did beseech you by us: we pray for you in Christ's stead, be ye reconciled to God. For He hath made Him to be sin for us, who knew no sin; that we might be made the righteousness of God in Him."[32]

---

[30] 2 Corinthians 5:17 NKJV
[31] Galatians 3:28-29 NKJV
[32] 2 Corinthians 5:18-21 KJV

Thus, Christ has given us the resources to expose the big "lie" and defeat it in our lives and in our churches. We are confronted by the lie every time we turn on the television, or other social media. While there are many prominent individuals in position to promote public persuasion in the world, I pray that they will not let the lie reign in their hearts.

Anything that dismantles Christian influence and enhances the left's power is deemed as progressive.

Secular progressivism is described by Benjamin Wiker as "the steady removal of Christianity from the center of culture." Radical progressivism loves to profane -what is sacred and to "reject Christianity itself by destroying anything that could lead to it." Anything that dismantles Christian influence and enhances the left's power is deemed as, progressive. As ambassadors of Christ, we must counter this with the Gospel Truth! We speak to this deception only the true message from Christ.

STUDY GUIDE: WORKSHEET AND REFLECTIONS
CHAPTER 7

1. Jesus promised, "I will ask the Father, and He will give you another Helper, to be with you _____, even the Spirit of _____ …"

2. As a seed contains the full potential of the tree, so the contains the full potential of the _____. Likewise, the church of Jesus Christ has the great potential power with the Holy Spirit _____ of us.

3. The Book of Acts is the only book in the Bible with no ending, it is still being written concerning the _____ of the _____, the church (His present-day disciples).

4. One of the most severe warnings ever issued in all history by the Lord Jesus to adults who _____ _____.

5. When we can see ourselves in the light of the biblical narrative, forsaking false cultural definitions, and the traditions of men, we can see the redemptive _____ of God reaching out through _____ _____ into a lost and broken _____.

6. Secular progressivism is described as the steady removal of _____ from the center of culture.

7. Anything that dismantles Christianity _____ and enhances the Left's power is deemed as _____.

Chapter Eight

THE GOAL OF SPIRITUALITY

Many today are asking, "what is God doing through the church? What is His purpose in all of this? The apostle Paul's great statement of the end result of God's strategy for the human race. God's goal, says Paul, is that,

"We come to the unity of the faith and of the knowledge of the Son of God, to a perfect man, to the measure of the stature of the fulness of Christ; that we should no longer be children, tossed to and fro and carried about with every wind of doctrine, by the trickery of men, in the cunning craftiness of deceitful plotting, but speaking the truth in love, may grow up in all things into Him who is the head – Christ – from the whole body, joined and knit together by what every joint supplies, according to the effective working by which every part does its share, causes growth of the body for the edifying of itself in love." (Ephesians 4:13-16 NKJV) Emphasis added.

Notice, two times in this passage, the apostle gives us the ultimate goal of the "life of faith." It is the standard by which we can judge our progress as Christians. In verse 13 he says it is "the measure of the stature of the fulness of Christ." And in verse 15 he urges us to "grow up in all things into Him who is the head – Christ." He also makes it clear "perfect man" means "mature manhood!" Thus, God's ultimate goal for us is, "to be conformed to the image of His Son" (see Romans 8:29). Adult men and women, GEN Y's and Gen Zers who demonstrate the character qualities of His Son – Jesus Christ.

But sadly, today much of the church has chosen not to give God what He requires (Bible standards of holiness and truth), but what they want to give Him (by their human standards of science, reason, and relativism). God's desires are for you and me to fulfill our humanity, the design that He intended when He created Adam and Eve. He does not want a church filled with theological authorities, but He wants ordinary people who bear the fruit of the in-dwelling Holy Spirit and faithfulness of Jesus Christ!

BIBLICAL LITERACY

Biblical literacy, is the believer's ability to know God's heart and mind, having been opened upon regeneration to know the Scriptures:

- How to use them to *experience* His transforming power personally.
- How to share them with others so they may *experience* Him also (see Luke 24:44-49).
- The goal of Biblical literacy is not to win a debate, but to win souls from all nations (As Christ builds His Church, the body of Christ), through the power of the Holy Spirit and the Word of God working in tandem.

BIBLICAL KNOWLEDGE

The intent of *Biblical knowledge* then is to impact those in darkness, drawing them to repentance of sin and trust in Christ for the forgiveness of sins that they may become members of the body of Christ. Whether you are facing an atheist, postmodernist, human secularist, Muslim, or New Ager, Jehovah Witness, the goal of the biblically literate believer must be able to share the gospel of

Jesus Christ and answer questions about our hope in Christ with humility and reverence. The apostle Peter encourages, *"but in your hearts honor Christ the Lord as holy, always being prepared to make a defense to anyone who asks you for a reason for the hope that is in you; yet do it with gentleness and respect."* (1 Peter 3:15 ESV)

Additionally, biblical literacy in the life of the new converted believer through the power of the Holy Spirit is to remove the remnants of *fleshly* attitudes and *ungodly* acts and actions that ruled in our hearts and minds as nonbelievers (see Romans 6:12-14; Ephesians 2:1-3). The born again from above believer is now indwelt by the Holy Spirit to teach the Word of God that he or she may be transformed by the Spirit's power and the Word working in tandem to live a life pleasing to God. We now have the mind of Christ (see 1 Corinthians 2:16).

SPIRITUAL MATURITY

Second, biblical literacy, in the life of the born-again believer is spiritual maturity (see 1 Peter 2:1-3; James 1:22-25). It is important for those both in the body and outside the body to recognize the gospel's *power* to transform a person's life for God's purposes (in any generation in any era). The apostles after the Day of Pentecost, the coming and indwelling of the Holy Spirit are the model examples for us.

Be it known, spiritual maturity does not come from just knowing the verses by rote (head knowledge) from the Bible – but by internalizing and applying them to transform us. The Word of God challenges and replaces the old self dependent, fleshly nature with the transformed life by the power of the gospel. The apostle Paul says,

"But I say to you walk by the Spirit and you will not gratify the desires of the flesh. For the desires of the flesh are against the Spirit, and the desires of the Spirit are against the flesh, for these are opposed to each other, to keep you doing the things you want to do, but if you are led by the Spirit, you are not under the law.

Now the works of the flesh are evident: sexual immorality, impurity, sensuality, idolatry, sorcery, enmity, strife, jealousy, fits of anger, rivalries, dissensions, envy, drunkenness, orgies, and things like these. I warn you before, that those who do such things will not inherit the kingdom of God." (Galatians 5:16-21 ESV) Emphasis added throughout.

But the fruit of the Spirit is: love, joy, peace, patience, kindness, goodness, self-control; against such things there is no law. And those who belong to Christ Jesus **have crucified the flesh** with its passions and desires" (Galatians 5:22-24 ESV) Christians are spiritually *"crucified with Christ."*

The **power of the Word of God** working in tandem with the **Holy Spirit** continually transform **us into His image** so that our transformation can validate the good news we share with those outside of the body of believers:

"And we all, with unveiled face, beholding the glory of the Lord, are being transformed into the same image from one degree of glory to another. For this comes from the Lord who is the Spirit." (2 Corinthians 3:18 ESV)

Just because a believer is exposed to sound doctrine and truth in theology does not guarantee that the believer will become biblically literate. Even though the Corinthian church had access to some of the best Bible teachers of that day [Paul, Peter, and Apollos] they were still carnal and struggling with becoming truly biblically-literate. Their failure to understand God's Word and His will led many to moral shipwreck – which eventually leads to the failure of their spiritual witness.

Another glowing example of what is expected for *all* believers is to be biblically literate as was a Christian married couple named Aquila and Priscilla, mere tentmakers. However, we meet them in Acts 18 where Apollos, an Alexandrian who is noted for being a great Bible teacher but limited to John's baptism. Aquila and Pricilla pulled Apollos to the side and explained to him the way of Christ more accurately.`

Have we fallen short in a similar manner? We likewise fall short, while being exposed to the best preachers and teachers of our day. We can overcome this failure and achieve by confronting our fleshly ways and surrender to the Holy Spirit to change "me" through the application of God's Word in our lives.

ALL THINGS NEW

People typically evaluate Christ or anyone else according to the flesh. However, in 2 Corinthians 5:17-19, Paul is presenting the results of Christ's death for the spiritual believer and their death with Christ. All things are new because the believer's life is being transformed into the likeness of Christ. Because of Christ's death and resurrection, His satisfaction of God's righteous demands – God is *now* able to turn toward us.

God has made us new creatures *in Christ* and has given us the ministry of reconciliation, meaning "a change of relation from enmity to peace." We who have been reconciled to God have the privilege of telling others that they can be reconciled to Him as well. While all Christians are expected to evangelize – all do not have the gift of evangelist, however,

- Any Christian should be able to share (their testimony) to others of what happened when he or she became a Christian. The apostle Peter says, a Christian should, *"be ready always to give …. a reason of the hope that is in you."* (I Peter 3:15 KJV)
- Witnessing should be as easy as talking about meaningful life experiences. If you can talk about how wonderful your mate, children, and grandchildren are – you can witness for Christ.
- In fact, many Christians (both women and men) today are stepping up to the plate. Evangelism can be done anywhere (so pray on).

Certainly, these post-coronavirus, high prices, politics, systemic racism, rising rent, Gen Zers mental health problems, and many other concerns such as the war in Eastern Europe, rising terrorist attacks in Jerusalem, daily heat, tornados, fires, blizzards, and floods across America has set many looking for answers

Anyone of the above-mentioned crisis should be enough to drive all of us to realize just how frail and fluid our lives are from day to day. People are crying, "I need help!" Are we listening saints? Jesus Christ came 2000 years ago for such a time as this, but He has chosen, His Body, the Church to be the means for the Spirit to operate through (individually and corporately)! There is a Word from the Lord!

SPIRIT-FILLED FOR THE JOURNEY

When Jesus went back to the Father, He sent back the Holy Spirit, whose role is to reproduce the life of Jesus Christ in the believer. Therefore, Jesus is able to say that the church will do greater works than He Himself did upon the earth – because in reality it is not the church nor the individual Christian that's doing those works. Rather those works are being done by a risen, ascended Lord through the Holy Spirit, working within and through the body of Christ, the Church. Give Him, "Praise and Glory!" He is worthy to be praised!

STUDY GUIDE: WORKSHEET AND REFLECTIONS
CHAPTER 8

1. Read Ephesians 4:13-16, notice two times in the passage the apostle gives us the ultimate goal of the life of faith:

    1. _____.

    2. _____.

2. He makes it clear "perfect man" means "mature manhood." Thus, God's ultimate goal for us is to_____.
(see Romans 8:29).

3. Today much of the church has chosen not to give God what He requires _____ _____ of holiness and truth. But to give Him what they desire to give by human standards of: _____, _____, and _____.

4. God wants ordinary people who bear the fruit of the _____ _____ _____ and faithfulness of Jesus Christ.

5. First, the intent of _____ knowledge is to impact those in _____, drawing them to repentance of sin and trust in Christ for the forgiveness of sins that they may become members of the body of Christ.

6. Secondly, biblical literacy, in the life of the born-again believer is _____ _____ (see 1 Peter 2:1-3; James 1:22-25).

7. When Jesus went back to the Father, He sent back the _____ _____, whose role is to _____ the life of Christ in the believer.

Chapter Nine

THE UNITY OF THE SAINTS

"… But, speaking the truth in love, may grow up in all things into Him who is the head – Christ – from whom the whole body, joined and knit together by what every joint supplies, which every part does its share, causes growth of the body for the edifying of itself in love." (Ephesians 4:15-16 NKJV)

One of the most destructive forces in the church today is conflict between Christians. Division among brothers and sisters has destroyed lives and homes, destroyed churches, and disgraced the gospel of Jesus Christ. Paul stresses the need for Christian unity. He exhorted the Ephesian Christians to be "eager to maintain the unity of the Spirit in the bond of peace" (Ephesians 4:3 KJV). This is one among a number of Scriptures that advocate the need for Christian agreement. It is unreal for Christians to act like there are no differences among them. There is absolutely no group in the world so gloriously diverse and heterogeneous as the church. The genius of the church is that it is made up of many different kinds of people.

In the true church of Jesus Christ, the rich and poor gather on the same footing, without distinction, in Christ between Jews and Gentiles, men or women, black, brown, white, or any other color (see

1 Corinthians 12:13; Galatians 3:28; Colossians 3:11; James 2:1-6). This certainly is not the way the church is, but this is the way church was meant to be and can be. The church crosses all the boundaries we construct.

Also weaved into Paul's message to the Ephesian church is a powerful implication. Despite the differences between the early Christians – there is also a basic underlying unity. Please know, this unity *is not* produced by the believers. Having said that, nowhere does the apostle tell the believers that they should strive to produce unity. Instead, he admonishes them to *maintain the unity that is already there.*

The church is never told to create unity.

The church is *never* told to create unity. There is a unity that exists in the church by virtue of the simple fact that the church exists. We human beings are incapable of producing this unity which is so necessary to the life of the church. It can only be produced by the Spirit of God. But once produced, Christians are *responsible* to maintain it. And maintain this unity through Christlike love. Jesus commanded us to "love one another." The unionists try to manufacture a semblance of unity, but not the true unity of the Spirit, but an outward union of Christians. Unity is a godly and spiritual characteristic. Union is an institutional, worldly concoction. Again, unity is something God produces, and we maintain both individually and corporately. Union is something humans construct out of their own fleshly efforts. Many churches settle for a union (organizational) semblance of the true unity. That is why Paul takes great effort to make sure there is no misunderstanding of the true nature of the unity of the Spirit he wrote,

"There is one body, and one Spirit, just as you were called in one hope of your calling, one Lord, one faith, one baptism, one God and Father of all, who is above all, and through all, and in you all." (Ephesians 4:4-6 NKJV)

Notice in the passage above, Paul presents a sevenfold unity:

- one body
- *one Spirit*
- one hope
- *one Lord*
- one faith
- one baptism
- *one God*

Here is the true unity of the body of Christ, we see God's answer to Jesus' prayer in Gethsemane: "That they may be *one*; even as thou, Father, art in me, and I in thee." (John 17:21 KJV) Emphasis added. It is true that a body is an organization, but here the body is so much more. The body of Christ consists of thousands of cells *with one mutually shared life* – bound together as an organism in bodily unity. Herein is the *mystery* or secret of the body – *all parts share one life together.* As my wife and I traveled the globe in ministry, we learned to recognize the basic unity of the Spirit which already exists among true Christians.

No matter the theological, political, geographical, cultural, or racial differences between us and other believers, the mutual life in Christ is immediately evident. Even in these trying times in this country – there remains a sense of belonging to each other. The shared love and Spirit of God within us will not allow any thoughts or things that might try to interrupt or break the unity of the Spirit. Praise God!

ACCORDING TO PATTERN

As the world moves on through the twenty-first century and third millennium, we must become the kind of Church that God intended us to be from the beginning. We must become the kind of Christians God intended; therefore, we must learn and teach others the practice of deep love and fellowship (*koinonia*). We must practice what is called, one another ministries, some fifty statements recorded throughout the New Testament: i.e., carrying one another's burdens, sharing one another's hurts and deep disappointments, confessing our faults one to another, rejoicing with one another, and encouraging one another while maintaining the unity of the Spirit.

Winds of change are whistling all around the world. Humanity Is squirming with unrest and rebellion everywhere. Our political institutions have totally ignored God's moral law for political correctness' sake. Division has become the norm so, it seems that polarization is all we understand now in politics, to the right or to the left with little or no wiggle room in between.

The *way* of the gun has viciously increased in all corners of this country, with a demonic fury never seen before. With daily shootings at random, unprovoked physical attacks, and many other atrocities, we are clearly seeing that there is a thin line separating civilization from anarchy. Physical threats and vicious criticism among politicians seem to win votes today.

Today the line between civilization and anarchy is so blurred, many of our political leaders are caving into anarchy, if necessary, even carrying with them some of this country's most respected religious leaders. Sadly, many people have counted the church out as irrelevant today. Is that true? Can the church make a difference in this dangerous and upside-down world? The mixed church of true and false people in the kingdom of heaven in Matthew 13, Mark 4 depicts what is visible to the world of the church that exists on earth between the two advents of Christ.

However, the true Church, the body of Christ, is alive and well on planet Earth. Those who study God's Word know that there will be a "falling away" during this period. But at the same time the true Church will be anxiously awaiting the Coming of Christ for His true Church. Matthew records how the seed (Word) was accepted and rejected in the world during the absence of the King. Rather than a great harvest of souls as many prophesies, larger and larger portions of the world population are actually rejecting the Word, especially in the United States and other countries of the Western world. Secularism (No God, No Christ, No Holy Spirit, "No true Word of truth" and "No true believers wanted") is spreading like wildfire.

Only *one quarter* of the "seeds" (Word) *sown* in the world between the two Advents were able to *"bear fruit"* to the Glory of God (see Mark 3-8). Notice as you read through the passage, Jesus' parables go beyond mere entertainment or moralizing; they teach vital spiritual truths about the kingdom of heaven. The point of the parable is that the condition of the ground (the heart of each person) determines the potential for growth. Those who have become complacent and lackadaisical are not likely to receive the Word with benefit.

A mystery in Scripture is a truth God has revealed or will reveal at appropriate time.

The apostle Paul in Rome jailed under false pretenses looked about seeing the decadent life of that city, and the debauchery of moral corruption in Ephesus was legendary. The city was the center of worship for the sex goddess, Diana of the Ephesians. The Christians of first century Ephesus faced similar problems and asked the same questions.

Cruelty wise, the Roman legions were ready to march anywhere to suppress any rebellion or civil disorder. Seeing the decadent life in the city of Rome and knowing the conditions of the life in the city of Ephesus. Paul was in a Roman jail chained day and night to a guard, awaiting his appearance before Nero. What would Paul tell the Ephesian Christians to do? Notice his striking answer, are we listening?

"I therefore, a prisoner for the Lord, urge you to walk in a manner worthy of the calling to which you have been called, with all humility and gentleness, with patience, bearing with one another in love, eager to maintain the unity of the Spirit in the bond of peace. There is one body and one Spirit – just as you were called to the one hope that belongs to your call." (Ephesians 4:1-4 ESV)

What does the apostle say to the Ephesian church in light of so many desperate cries of human needs? What is his answer to the pleas of justice and relief from oppression all around him?

According to pattern, Paul advises: *"Fulfill your calling! Obey your orders! Don't deviate from the divine strategy! Follow your Lord!"* In this admonition the apostle clearly recognizes the true nature and function of the church (then and today). Paul, the apostle to the Gentiles, in his defense of faith insisted that faith and works are not enemies. True faith and righteous works go hand in hand. They are two parts of God's work in us. Faith brings a person to salvation, and works are the effect. Amen!

SUPPORT YOUR LOCAL CHURCH

Gallup recently reported that for the first time in America's history less than half the population claimed to have a faith. A deeper study reveals that the majority of this reduction among the churches has accelerated in the past twenty years. In 2000, 70% of the nation claimed a faith – by 2020 that number fell to 47%. With fewer people claiming any faith – churches are closing across this nation at a phenomenal rate. In the past, although thousands of churches close each year – the loss was always offset by new church plants opening. Statistically, that pattern flipped in 2014 when for the first time *more churches closed than opened.* Every year since, that gap has continued to widen with more churches closings and fewer new ones opened.

According to Lifeway Research, 4500 Protestant Churches closed in 2019, the last data available with about 3000 new churches opening. It was the first time the number of churches in the United States had not grown since the Evangelical firm started studying the topic. Also, with the pandemic speeding up, a broader trend of Americans turning away from Christianity, researchers say to closures will only have accelerated. Even if we didn't have this data, you must admit that America is not the same! The deterioration has increased at an astounding rate. Many of those remaining are on life support! With every church closure – America becomes a little darker!

"Fulfill your calling! Obey your orders! Don't deviate from the divine strategy! Follow your Lord!"

The Apostle Paul

One of the most powerful entities in creation is the church. It was born on the streets of Jerusalem at Pentecost. One of the first considerations should be:

- Study the early church models in the Book of Acts, what the church was intended to be.
- Reestablish (regroup) your prayer ministry in the local church.
- Realize that the "call to pray" is to every member of the church – everyone is on the battlefield.
- Pray fervently for your pastor and home church.
- We need to fully support our home church.
- We need to provide mentoring, resources and emergency funds for churches that need help.
- Support our home church with our time, talent, and resources.
- We need to populate our churches by inviting those far from God to join us.
- Finally, many churches found small groups to be a blessing during the church lockdown.

WHAT WE FACE TODAY (BIBLICAL AND SPIRITUAL FAMINE)

We must guard our theology. During the Covid epidemic many things changed. One big change in the culture was the tremendous awareness of spiritual famine in the land. President Biden claimed during his campaign that we are in a battle for the soul of America. The American Christian Church must acquire the 1st church's vigor and vitality as we battle for the *souls of Americans!* The situation is critical! Our hearts are easily *drawn away from God and His Word.*

The people have a habit of losing interest for God's truth. Except for a grace-driven effort, people don't just gravitate toward godliness, prayer, obedience to Scripture, faith, and delighting themselves in the Lord.

- We drift toward compromise and call it tolerance.
- We drift to disobedience and call it freedom.
- We drift toward paganism and the other isms and call it faith.
- We drift into indiscipline of lose self-control and call it relaxation.
- We drift into prayerlessness and say we are escaping legalism.

BIBLICALLY THIRSTY

To understand the seriousness of this biblical famine that is swiftly approaching we need to dig into its implications:

1. According to Barna Research, "the most critical is how many of our churches are adapting *unbiblical beliefs.*"
2. Traditional emphasis of seeing the Bible as the infallible, inerrant Word of God has been relaxed, and many Christians today share the same criticisms about the Bible as the atheist, secularist, humanist, and the postmodernist.
3. The report goes on to say, "52% or 5 out 10 Christians do not believe in objective moral truth.
4. Additionally, 4 out of 10 Christians *do no read* the Bible.

As a pastor and Bible Teacher, I am truly concerned about the wayward theological patterns trending in churches everywhere. Many churches are going too far relaxing their doctrines, and in compromising biblical truth to reach *disinterested* groups. For many, many centuries, God's Word has been the center of Christian preaching!

Today, questioning scriptural authority is fashionable even in some faith communities. Processing God's Word through cultural filters has become the "in-thing" for an assortment of popular speakers. First, God turns His back on us. In Romans 1:18-32, we find God giving people over to their sinful wills. Even in our churches and homes no doubt many people can attribute their *sufferings* to their desire to divorce themselves from the Word of God.

[Mark Twain once defined a literary classic, "A book which people praise and don't read." Isn't it sad, that describes the way many people in our society approach the Bible].

SPIRITUALLY EMPTY

Sadly, we distinguish Pentecostals and Charismatics from other believers by their insistence on the *experiential* power of the Holy Spirit. While most Christians make allowances for the Spirit's activity, often attributing His supernatural presence to an almost passive power slowly at work in our lives. Like a giant iceberg inching its way through the ocean, with an expected time of arrival to be a thousand years from now, the Holy Spirit moves us – yet His effects are almost imperceptible. Someone described the move of the Spirit in this case as comparing one digging a ditch with a large tablespoon versus one using an entrenching machine. No comparison!

Of late, current Christian culture, even current Pentecostal and Charismatic culture, seems to be following the same path with *traditionally held beliefs* regarding the Spirit's activity. Sadly, teaching now takes the center position – experience and encounter are placed in a spot after the meeting or shoved off into a side room somewhere as to not disrupt what the center-point of the service is really about. So, meeting after meeting go on traditionally with little or no change; and most people simply encounter another sermon.

While current traditional cultural Christianity often drifts toward formalism with a focus on *information,* unashamedly charismatic and Pentecostal emphasizes *the transformative power* of the Holy Spirit – giving space and time for the power of the Holy Spirit to move:

"For by one Spirit we were all baptized into one body – whether Jews or Greeks, whether slaves or free – and have all been made to drink into one Spirit. For in fact the body is not one member but many." (1 Corinthians 12:13-14 NKJV)

Every service seems to be supplied with a speaker or minister who carries a tangible anointing of the Spirit of God – and impacts with signs and wonders. The Holy Spirit has a supernatural life waiting for every believer.

THE SPIRIT AND THE WORD

We have people on both sides of the aisle in the matter. One side argues for experience only, while others prefer teaching only. Oh, how beautiful, helpful and obedient it is to allow both working in tandem! And being assembled together with them, He commanded them not to depart from Jerusalem, but to wait for the *promise* of the Father, "which," He said, "You have heard from Me:

For John baptized with water, but you shall be baptized with the Holy Spirit not many days from now." (Acts 1:5 NKJV)

The passive promise tense of the verb indicates that baptism does not depend on our efforts to obtain the promise. The Greek word for *baptized* means "to immerse" or "to dip." Further Spirit baptism means we have been identified with Jesus Christ and placed in *spiritual union* with one another in the body of Jesus Christ, the church. (see 1 Corinthians 12:12, 13)

"But you shall receive power when the Holy Spirit has come upon you; and you shall be witnesses to Me in Jerusalem, and in all Judea and Samaria, and to the end of the earth." (v. 8 NKJV)

The disciples were told to "wait" which means what they were assigned to do would require more than human strength; this was power for a new task – to take the gospel to the ends of the earth. Be My witnesses! As I stated in an earlier section, the Book of Acts has no ending as the other books of the Bible. That means the Spirit is still writing today through us, the body of Christ! As I stated earlier, the Book of Acts is more than a history book – it is the main "Operations Manual" for the body of Christ, the church on earth between the two advents. The Holy Spirit is the Chief operating Officer – without Him, there can be no viable Church operations! Our life (growth) is on the resurrection side of the cross. *Study prayerfully John 14-16 and Matt. 28:19-20, Ephesians 4, 1 Corinthians 12, Romans 1-8.*

A little lesson from children's church: "Read your Bible and pray every day – and you'll grow, grow, grow. Don't read your Bible and pray every day and you'll shrink, shrink, shrink. Amen.

STUDY GUIDE: WORKSHEET AND REFLECTIONS
CHAPTER 9

1. One of the most destructive forces in the church today is conflict _____ _____.

2. This division among the brethren has destroyed lives and homes, destroyed churches, and disgraced the gospel of Jesus Christ. Paul stresses the need for _____ _____ in the church.

3. There is absolutely no group so gloriously diverse and heterogeneous as the church. The genius of the church is that it is made up of many different kinds of people. Study carefully 1 Corinthians 12:13; Galatians 3:28; Colossians 3:11; James 2:1-6). Is this the way God meant the church to be? Explain your conclusion:

4. Despite the differences between the early Christians – there is an underlying unity. Please know, this unity is not produced by the members. Where or who is the source? Explain your response:

5. To be the Christians God intended us to be – we must learn and practice _____ love and _____ (koinonia).

6. The NIV Bible lists some fifty what I call "one another ministries" that we must practice while maintaining the unity of the Spirit. For example, we are to "love one another" "carry one another's burdens" "confessing our faults to one another." Review Chapter 8 and follow 2 Timothy 2:2.

7. The mixed church of true and false Christians in the kingdom of heaven in Matthew 13 and Mark 4 depicts what is visible to the world of the church that exists on earth between the two _____ of Christ.

Chapter Ten

THE MUSTNESS OF
THE MISSION

"And all that generation were gathered to their fathers. And there arose another generation after them who did not know the LORD or the work that He had done for Israel." (Judges 2:10 ESV)

For many years the preoccupation of the Black Church has historically been to confront the scars, and wounds of African American people. Today however, a couple of new generations of African Americans, the Millennials and the Gen Zers arose who do not know the bridge that brought us over the troubled waters of the past. Too many of them think the church is outdated, impotent, and irrelevant or so says the secular culture.

Therefore, many of or young people are exploring cults, religious sects, and *new* ideologies. They have turned to money, education, social media, and peers for the answers the church once provided. Today the Black church must welcome their innovative expressions and converse with this generation. At the same time, we *must* introduce the Spirit- illuminating and transforming truth of the Gospel.

Relativism (another philosophy)

I believe one positive from the coronavirus epidemic came as a by-product, a counter to run-away relativism.[33] The "screen" has provided the smallest local churches, and the five-fold ministers of Ephesians 4:11 a platform and open door. I spent five years in Europe during the sixties, three years in Germany and two years in France (1959 – 1964). My point in all of this is, I use to listen to Radio-Free Europe and the struggle those pioneers in that day getting truth to the Nations that were closed to the Gospel, behind the so-called "Iron Curtain" (Communism), however, today the communists have lost their struggle to keep the Internet at bay with their citizens.

The availability of technology during COVID-19 lock down has created a world where we are connected. The world is smaller through technology. Bread of life has been a blessing for so many over the past twenty-five years of making disciples, establishing churches and ministries, but during the COVID-19 epidemic social sights where introduced to the ministry: Facebook, blogs, YouTube, around the world. I have written and published eighteen books, hundreds of lectures and manuscripts, grasped many other opportunities to level the playing field *so that any one of us can have a spiritual part and voice!* Emphasis added.

The opportunity for expansion to spread the Gospel probably has never been better. These opportunities do not end only with the screen. You can hop on a plane and fly to the other side of the world in a few hours. There is room for you! While the world has grown smaller and people are more exposed as I said earlier, to other religions, cultures, and philosophies of life – it give *relativism,* a belief that truth is not absolute, but relative, the opportunity to rise above the roofs – and it is doing just that! This view expresses itself as, *"What is true for you may not be true for me."*

---

[33] Relativism is a family of philosophical views which deny claims to objectivity within a particular domain and asserts that facts in that domain are relative to the perspective of an observer or the context in which they are assessed. Assessed 6/1/22 https://wwwmerriam-webster.com/dictionary/relativism.

This philosophical view thrived during the first century. In fact, Pontus Pilate summarized it best when he asked Jesus, *"What is truth?"* As more people fall into this view the casualty rate goes up rapidly. Most people especially since COVID-19, and now war in Ukraine, inflation, food and gas prices, housing, and discrimination are showing signs of wear and tear. As fear has hit the world hard. We are experiencing a yearning inside for something more substantial that relativism *cannot* satisfy.

It takes only a little time under relativism for life to lose all meaning and darkness and despair consumes all of one's thoughts. Living under such a philosophy of life drives one to search for more solid ground on which to stand. The despair it brings creates a favorable climate for the Good News of the kingdom of God.

Paganism And The Occult

The apostle Paul was met with many false idols even one to the unknown god in Athens which provoked him to much grief (see Acts 17:22-23). He took advantage of the prevailing religious curiosity. On Mars Hill he presented *the true* Creator to the epicurean and stoic philosophers of that day. Later, in Lystra Paul and Barnabas were worshipped as gods, and stoned the same day.

False Religions, Cults, And Spiritism

Things that use to be fun and funny in comic books and other fiction such as vampires, goths, spirits, and superhumans have become subcultures of our society. Sadly, they are becoming a part of the people's lives. There is virtually a religious cult, form, or deity for everyone in the kingdom of this world. The spirit of Babylon (world) provides a variety of deceptive options – you chose!

With each group and false religion launched by Satan, the goal is to keep people away from the true God, the true Jesus Christ, the true Holy Spirit, and the true gospel. Is there any wonder that

Scripture exhorts Christians everywhere to **"beware of Satan's schemes"** (see 2 Corinthians 2:11).

Rapidly growing among young people today are the practicing of "New Age"[34] witchcraft, occult worship, and paganism.[35] They long to experience the spirit world that they certainly know exists.

Just as in Paul's day as he traveled throughout the Roman Empire – today people are worshipping many gods, seeking spiritual enlightenment, and power. The Scripture says, we have the same Spirit within us (believers) that raised Jesus from the dead. We can make the true power and experience of the true kingdom of God *attractive* to people, just like it was in Ephesus when Paul brought the kingdom there.

Through reading the history of Rome, drunken orgies stand out as one of the favorite past times. Most people believe that the dissolving moral foundation was the cause of the unraveling of the Roman Empire. Sexual perversion (unlocked and peddled by the spirit of Babylon) in this country and the world in the (1960s) is running rampart. There are many side effects to this increase in sexual activity to include:

- STD's
- AIDS
- Unwanted pregnancies
- Abortions
- Trafficking of young girls and women
- Women held as sex slaves
- Fatherless children
- Little respect for authority
- Divorce

---

[34] Behind today's mantra, "I'm spiritual but not religious." They reject formalized expressions of religion for inner enlightenment. Peter Jones, *The Other Worldview* (Kirkdale Press 2015) 87-89.

[35] Paganism, a modern religious movement incorporating beliefs and practices specifically nature worship. Assessed 6/1/22, https://wwwmeriamwebster.com/dictionary.

- Sexual perversion
- Sexual bondage
- Sexual throw-aways
- Broken homes
- Battered wives and children
- Loss of employment
- Drug and alcohol abuse
- Despair
- Suicide

Believers in the early church found the bondage of sexual immorality to be very challenging. Sexual perversion always leaves broken and used people all over the landscape. A life of sexual bondage, abandoned sexual partners, and cohabitation consumes many souls. Such sins fill them with darkness, sickness, and eventually death. These painful realities and difficult challenges also – present us (the body of Christ) with great ministry opportunities. I could go on, but this is enough to demonstrate how many cultic groups and false religions have come about through demonic spirits.

Scripture warns us that Satan can masquerade as an angel of light, seeking to deceive you (see 2 Corinthians 11:14). First John 4:1 admonishes believers to *"test the spirits."* There are many false revelations coming from wicked spirit teachers today, and we must test these teachings against the Scriptures, which are inspired by the Holy Spirit, the "Spirit of truth" (see John 14:17; 15:26; 16:13).

Without a doubt, recent statistics prove that false religions and cults have deceived myriads of people. Islam boasts more than 1.8 billion adherents (fastest growing religion in the world), encompassing over 24% of the earth's population.

SHIFTING VALUES

I pray that we are seeing something gigantic equal to or surpassing the past Great Awakenings, and the Azuza street revivals of 1906. People coming to Christ where people are sincere about a right relationship with Him and a deeper spiritual life. We've spoken much concerning culture thus far. Culture is defined as a collective assent of people living within the boundaries of their shared values.

Sadly, many individuals in this country have forfeited their eternal value with Christ for a portion of earthly (temporary values) here with humankind. So called values that exclude other people who don't look like them. I pray that our church cultures are noticing how various groups of people that we reject through their own personal or inherited value systems, church constitutions and bylaws are the very kind of people that Jesus Christ, our Savior embraced.

Many of our churches need to do in house evangelism with the same exuberance they have used for those on the outside. I have been shunned by many of the brethren because I am a registered (kingdom) Independent, rather than a Democrat or Republican. Oh! If we could get that worked up about the kingdom of God – we could move the world (the spirit of Babylon).

FAR FROM GOD

I think we forget sometimes that American politics are of this world. Our first allegiance is to the kingdom of God! The Problem with our country today is we've moved "far" from God. We have become self-centered rather than Christ-centered. Christ is the center, but we have created our own manmade orbits. We have moved so far from God, that He is no longer near. Yet, He hasn't moved. We moved!

One of the problem with America today is that we the people, have turned too quickly and landed in an orbit between God and other things that we now look to in His place. Now, rather than repent and let God do what only God can do – bring us back to center! As a result, America is undergoing the consequences, whether through *active* or *passive wrath* because of our turning our backs and moving far away from God.

Our nation's problems are not just the results of corrupt politicians, inflation, epidemics, criminal violence, police brutality, racism, autonomy, extreme weather, climates out of control, burning forests around the compass, terrorists inside and outside of the country desiring to bring us down, and any number of other ills, to include not knowing our gender?

It has been said that America has sacrificed 63 million babies offered on the altar of personal pleasure, through the years to the god of abortion. Is there not a cause? A check of Scripture can be traced to the disobedient and ineffective Christians and churches! As I stated throughout this book God did not say the government was the salt of the earth nor the light of the world – but He did say the Church is both the light of the world and the salt of the earth (born again believers)! It is the churches responsibility to influence the culture, not the other way around. The problem today is not that sinners sin; that's what sinners do – sin! Since humankind is born in sin and shaped in iniquity (see Psalm 51:5; Ephesians 2:1-3).

The real problem is that the church (American Christianity) as a whole has failed to advance God's kingdom and principles in society in order to be *a positive influence* for good in America and the rest of the world.

In Joel 2, God sent His army of destruction to wake up *His people,* not to judge the rest of the world. God was Israel's problem Himself:

- God allowed the locusts to devour their crops.
- God allowed storms.
- God gave them over to the enemy.
- God was the aggressor – not the Philistines, not the Hittites. Just God! When God is the problem, then only God can be the solution.

And when God is the problem – only God can be the solution!

God's kingdom is *always countercultural* – standing *against* sinful values. The essence of the Gospel of the kingdom does not conform to any culture; it transcends the culture and at the same time transforms from within it.

Our mission is not to make the kingdom of God or its core message *bend* to the culture, but to position it in a way that is both appealing and unappealing at the same time.

Our mission is not to make the kingdom of God or its core message bend to the culture, but to position it in a way that is both appealing and unappealing at the same time. Values express how people *feel* about things and *what is important* to them.[36]

The church that grows from the soil of the culture will hopefully well represent the God-image values found within that culture but also stand in contrast to the evil values found there – and thereby be both appealing and unappealing. God is shifting the world for us to be more effective than we have ever been in the past.[37]

CHRISTIANITY TODAY

As I stated in an earlier section, we live in a time of extreme conflict and change in the church. Therefore, we need to be wise and alert to Satan's snares. We know that Satan has his own people, counterfeit Christians, in the church, standing ready to do his bidding. I noticed that the culture was winning the battle over same-sex marriages, and active homosexual lifestyles that go against truth of God's Word. But so does all sexual sins such as adultery, fornication, pedophilia, cohabitation, perversion and abuse. The Word of God has to be the point of separation! The world is doing its thing, sinning and tearing up foundations as they go.

---

[36] Neil Cole, *Church 3.0: upgrades for the future of the church* (Jossey-Bass Publisher 2010) 27

[37] Ibid. 109

Our culture wants the argument to be "the church versus the issue" which opens the door for negotiations. God has spoken, "Let the true Church say, "Amen!"

The Word of truth (Bible) has spoken, and the solution is clear, which means God has already spoken on the matter! With the fading of the biblical worldview, secular man is now king and soon he will be able to make or legislate whatever he wants and do whatever pleases him (what is wrong with that picture?). God is still in charge, and He has spoken! Hear Him pastors.

Recently, one denomination lost 34 churches because their denominational leadership decided to compromise and support the culture in areas of doctrine. Because these 34 churches chose to "*obey God rather than man.*" That denomination's leadership moved totally in the opposite direction of what the Word of God commands. Again, the culture's argument is for the church to agree, adjust their theology, and join them in condemning those who demand separation. Is this narrow thinking? Well the church went from house to house (small groups) during the first century. Many of our churches had their first taste of small group during the COVID epidemic. It was said of first century church, "They turned the world upside down." Much of the American church said after the closure, "Let's get back to normal!" As I stated earlier, perhaps we should think narrow and deeper rather than wider and shallower for our local Christian communities. Pastor did God change the paradigm in your church?

PRESSURE TO BOW TO CAESAR

Social scientists who are dedicated to reshaping America according to purely secular humanistic values agree that God and religion must be removed from government. The American Civil Liberties Union (ACLU) believes that God must be separated not only from government, but from every sphere of American life. Religion especially Christianity must be removed from government, from law, from education, and from the workplace.[38] With the public square free of any religious values, the door will be wide open for secular values to occupy:

- Cheapness of human life
- The promotion of all forms of immorality
- The sexualization of school children
- Pornography
- Religion designated as "private"
- Secularism is gradually being imposed upon society as the only viable point of view.
- Statism – is the notion that there is no power above the state to which it must be subject.
- The diminishing of individual freedoms.
- As the state removes our liberties – the spiritual "sphere" will continue to shrink, and our freedoms will slowly be cutoff.
- No one is able to run and hide.

I recently examined a report that stated, for the past couple of years reputable research has shown that, "many millennials are presently moving into celibacy as their lifestyle choice. Their reasoning stems from people not looking for relationship, but to them sex has become their only correspondence with a person. Therefore, increasing numbers of people are being more intentional about their celibacy. They surmise the word "abstinence" is more religious. Note their rationale for this:

1. To further develop their own personal self-love
2. Sex has become meaningless
3. Respect their autonomy
4. Better understand the type of relationship they want
5. So easy to fall into routine, doing what everyone else is doing without thinking about it.
6. I hope this will teach me to be more resilient, improve my self-respect.

---

[38] Janet L. Folger, *The Criminalization of Christianity* (Sisters, Oregon: Multnomah, 2005).

7. Build-up my self-esteem and confidence, set back and observe patterns and forge a new narrative for myself.
8. Change focus of what sex might really mean.
9. Many celebrates are joining them for example, since her separation from her husband in 2016, Drew Barrymore now 48, has practiced celibacy and has found that it enhanced in many ways the relationship in raising her two children.[39]

It is insanity to repeat the same method all the time – and expect a different result.[40] – Albert Einstein

---

Sharing the gospel is our primary responsibility since it only the cross of Christ that can transform the human heart. But once we are saved through Christ we must live out the applications of the cross in all areas of our life. We must strengthen (mature) individual Christians in our churches through the Spirit and the truths revealed in the Word of God, for the evil days to come.

I pray that pastors everywhere realize that the future of America will not rest on the shoulders of politicians, but on the fervent prayers of God's people as they share their faith as truthful and faithful witnesses to Christ who saved them!

---

[39] Assessed 1/17/23 https/www/independent/cu American ed/current newsletter.
[40] Ibid.

STUDY GUIDE: WORKSHEET AND REFLECTIONS
CHAPTER 10

1. Today, too many of the millennials and Gen Z generations think the _____, _____, and _____.

2. Therefore, they are exploring cults, religious sects, and new _____.

3. The availability of technology has made the world seem _____. In a sense we could say technically we are _____ _____.

4. Scripture warns us that Satan masquerade as an angel _____ _____ seeking to deceive you.

5. Culture is a collective assent of people living within the _____ of their shared values.

6. Sadly, many people in this country have forfeited their eternal value with Christ for a portion of _____ humankind.

7. God's kingdom is always _____ _____ standing against their sinful values.

Section Three

REACHING THE WORLD

Chapter Eleven

ARRESTED SPIRITUAL DEVELOPMENT

"For I Know the thoughts that I think toward you, says the LORD, thoughts of peace and not evil, to give you a future and a hope." (Jeremiah 29:11NKJV)

I begin this chapter with a shout out to the research projects and studies by Barna, Gallup, Pew and the many other such ministries dealing with the next generation. As a result of their meticulous work with tens of thousands, of teens, young adults, parents, pastors, other church leaders and Christian workers reveal how *young faith* can mature and thrive in even the darkest hour. We know a great deal about what is going wrong in the American church's efforts to connect with young Christians and non-Christians. There is hope, as the years of research passing on *lasting faith in Jesus Christ* in a culture increasingly hostile and indifferent toward Christianity.

Yet, the seeds of hope are germinating in the cracks, breaking through in many countries, places, and societies that are much more post-Christian than our nation. This confirms what Christianity has long recorded: The root of faithfulness often runs deeper in anxious and unsettled times, and sometimes in the darkest places. We see how this comes about in Jesus' parable of the Sower,

"A Sower went out to sow. And as he sowed, some seeds fell along the path, and the birds came and devoured them. Other seeds fell on rocky ground, where they did not have much soil, and immediately they sprang up, since they had no depth of soil, but when the sun rose, they were scorched. And since they had no root, they withered away. Other seeds fell among thorns, and the thorns grew up and choked them. Other seeds fell on good soil and produced grain, some a hundredfold, some sixty, some thirty. He who has ears let him hear." (Matthew 13:4-9 ESV)

The various kinds of soil illustrates the spiritual receptivity or resistance of the human heart, therefore, displaying a range of possible responses to the good news of God's kingdom. This parable has been a kind of guide to growth, to help Christians diagnose the condition of the soil (heart) they are working with.

As in that ancient story, today the soil of many hearts is rocky, dry, or filled with thistles, and weeds stifling out growth and life. Deep spiritual things that really matter most, which should be lovingly tended and skillfully cultivated, are choked to death by many hours of television, games, scrolling through social media and other pastime activities.

Many people turn daily to their screens for help in understanding this changing world. Young people use the screens in their pockets as counselors, entertainers, and instructors. They surmise, why should I worry about courage to stand before the pastor, parents, or teacher when you can just ask your cell phone and no one else needs to know? If not careful with our days so completely consumed that we may never get around to pursuing the deeper life in Christ. The virtual possibilities are virtually endless.

I believe Gen Z, and Y want and need more. And I believe the family of God, called the church can answer the stifled longings of not only this anxious age or any other age or era. In 1965, Dr. Martin Luther King Jr. in a sermon could have been talking about the present day when he asked, "How much of our modern life can be summarized in that arresting dictum of the poet Thoreau, 'Improved means to an unimproved end'? ... We have allowed our technology to outdistance our theology and for that reason we find ourselves caught up with many problems."[41]

We have allowed our technology to outdistance our theology and for this reason we find ourselves caught up with many problems.

– Dr. Martin Luther King Jr.

The church must: "Be strong in the Lord and in the strength of His might. Put on the whole armor of God, that you may be able to stand against the schemes of the devil. For our fight is not against flesh and blood, but against the rulers, against the authorities, against the cosmic powers over this present darkness, against the spiritual forces of evil in the heavenly places." (Ephesians 6:10-12 ESV)

Satan is using technology and governments as he believes he has humanity in his grasp. But remember, God, the Father "hath delivered us from the power of darkness, and hath translated us into the kingdom of His dear Son. In whom we have redemption through His blood, even the forgiveness of sins." (Colossians 1:13-14 KJV) Give Him praise and glory! God has placed His true Church here for such a time as this!

God helps us to overcome and live as the people He has created us to be, through His Spirit and His Word working in tandem within us. Remember His covenant promises to His church! Daily millions of Americans accept *compromising* ideas, behaviors, worship, and church that would have horrified all past generations. Followers of Jesus Christ in ages past chose to *obey* God rather than man!

---

[41] Dr. Martin Luther King Jr., from a sermon delivered at Temple Israel of Hollywood, February 26, 1965, accessed May 23, 2022. https://www.americanrhetoric.com/speeches/mlktempleisraelhollywood.htm.

GO ON TO PERFECTION! (MATURITY)

Standfast therefore in the liberty wherewith Christ hath made us free and be not entangled with the yoke of bondage. (Galatians 5:1) One of the greatest problems facing the church ever since its inception has been arrested spiritual development or progress toward maturity after conversion. This is a problem we need to move to the top of our list of spiritual priorities in the Body of Christ today. The great question is how we get such Christians interested in becoming more than the average mediocre Christian in their spiritual experience. The apostle Paul asked,

*"Ye did run well; who did hinder you that ye should not **obey** the truth?"* (Galatians 5:7 KJV)

So, the spiritual progress is slowed, arrested, going nowhere – this procession is accompanied by a lapse of moral dynamics, which **every** Christian should be aware of. Emphasis added. If we listen, we will hear God speaking:

"He that hath an ear, let him hear what the Spirit saith unto the churches." (Revelation 2:7 KJV).

I believe if you listen, we will hear the Spirit of the Living God say, "Let us go on to perfection:"

- Let us go beyond repentance from past sins.
- Let us get beyond forgiveness and cleansing.
- Let us go beyond the impartation of divine life.
- Let us be sure that we have absolute assurance.

Let's be clear, no deeper life can exist until life has been established. No progress can be made in the way until we are in the way. No growth can happen until there has been new birth. All effort toward a deeper spiritual life will only bring disappointment unless we have settled the matter of repentance from dead works, the forgiveness of sins, and the impartation of divine nature in regeneration. Two requirements of the individual to break the arrested spiritual development through obedience to the Word of God:

1. Living the sanctified life involves complete forsaking the world.
2. Additionally, living the sanctified life means turning fully to the Lord Jesus Christ.

This is emphasized in the Bible in the Old and New Testaments and is the standard that has been passed down from the early Apostolic Church. These two prerequisites can also be found written in the great hymns of the church and the great devotionals from the earliest days of the Church. This can be the experience of any Christian who wants to go on and break the arrested spiritual condition in his or her life and become a growing, moving, and dynamic disciple must adhere to these two requirements. This not only true with individual Christians, but it can be true of entire Christian communities.

Let Us Be Borne On

The writer of the letter to the Hebrews scolded them because of their spiritual dullness (see Hebrews 5:11-14); now he urges them to go on to perfection. The word perfection means (maturity). The writer has in mind "let us be borne or carried on." That is "carried on" borne by the Spirit – not talking about self-effort; he is appealing to the Hebrews (and us) to yield themselves to the Power of God. The same power that created and upholds the whole universe. How can we fall when God is holding us up?

However, rather than going ahead, these believers were tempted to repeat the same foundation that is described in (vv. 2-3). There are six principles of Christ in this foundation addressed to the Hebrew Christians but again (applicable to us). They wanted to return to Judaism as they faced the fires of persecution. These Hebrew Christians were tempted to "fall by the "wayside" by forsaking their committed/ confession to Christ (see 4:14; 10:23). They had already suffered from "arrested spiritual development," slipping back into "babyhood" (see Hebrews 5:11-14). They were now prone to return back to Judaism. He encouraged them not to lay again the foundation (see Hebrews 6:1-3):

- Repentance from dead works
- Have faith toward God
- The doctrine of baptism
- Laying on of hands
- Resurrection of the dead
- Eternal judgment

MOVING FORWARD AND UPWARD

It is imperative that the church today emphasize practical holiness (separation unto God) in all of life of every believer. In John 17:19, Jesus says He sanctified Himself. What He means is that He set Himself apart to serve God and through His atonement was able to set believers apart to serve and glorify God. It is essential that we thoroughly understand what all of this means, as not only our eternal destination depends on it – but the local churches' survival depends on it. In my book, *"We would see Jesus,"* I spent a whole chapter on this.[42] In Scripture sanctification is three-fold:

1. Positionally – the believer is seated with Christ in heaven (see John 17:16).
2. Practical – the believer has day-by-day victory over sin and grows in holiness [sanctified] and in likeness in Christ (see 1 John 5:4).
3. Perfect – "We shall be like Him for we shall see Him as He is" (see 1 John 3:1-2).[43]

---

42   Jay Leach, *We Would See Jesus* (Trafford Publishing, Bloomington, IN 2020) 74-75
43   Ibid. 76

GROW IN GRACE AND KNOWLEDGE

Peter admonishes all believers to: *"Grow in grace and knowledge of our Lord and Savior, Jesus Christ."* (2 Peter 3:18 ESV) His message to the Body of Christ today as it was to them is: Since you know the truth, then you should depart from the error of the wicked and grow in grace[44] and knowledge[45] of the Lord.

Our growth in grace depends on our growth in knowledge. The more we *know* about ourselves and Christ, the better we are able to grow spiritually and move forward in grace (favor of God). Where are you in your spiritual growth? Are you a babe in Christ, still living on milk and wandering in the wilderness of unbelief? Or are you maturing, feeding on the meat of the Word and making it a holy habit, practice (walk in and live in) the Word of God? One of the prominent themes of 2 Peter is his exhortation to all believers to attain a fuller more through knowledge of Jesus Christ (study 1:8; 2:20; 3:18).

44

[45] Knowledge (GK gnosis) this Greek word for knowledge connotes progressive, experiential, and personal knowledge; it is knowledge that can grow. We need to grow in our personal knowledge of Jesus Christ; such knowledge is the greatest protection against false teachings. Footnote: 2 Peter 3:18 NKJV.

STUDY GUIDE: WORKSHEET AND REFLECTIONS
CHAPTER 11

1. The various kinds of soil illustrates the spiritual receptivity or _____ of the human heart; therefore, displaying a range of possible responses to the _____ _____ of God's kingdom.

2. Satan, the prince of this world, uses technology and governments as he believes he has humanity in his grasp (carefully study Colossians 1:13-14).

3. Daily millions of Americans accept compromising ideas, behaviors, worship, and church that would have _____ all past generations.

4. The Spirit is saying to the churches, "Let's go on to _____."

5. No deeper life can exist until new life has been established.

6. Two requirements of the Christian can break the arrested spiritual development through _____ to the Word of God.

7. The two requirements are: (a) Living a holy life involves _____ the world and (b) Turning fully to the Lord Jesus Christ.

Chapter Twelve

A TIME OF CHANGE AND CONFLICT

"Beloved, do not think it strange concerning the fiery trial, which is to try you, as though some strange thing happened to you, but rejoice to the extent that you partake of Christ's sufferings, that when His glory is revealed, you may also be glad with exceeding joy. If you are reproached for the name of Christ, blessed are you, for the Spirit of glory and of God rests upon you. On their part He is blasphemed, but on your part He is glorified." (2 Peter 4:12-14 NKJV)

Our churches are deeply divided today on many issues, but none is more critical than Christianity. We live in a time of major conflict in the church. Millions of Christians are embracing an *"emerging"* new way of seeing Christianity. Millions of other Christians continue to embrace the old earlier vision of Christianity, often defending it as *"traditional"* Christianity – and determine that it is the legitimate way of being Christian.

I have struggled with different names to call these two ways of being Christian and have settled on *"traditional"* and the *"emerging"* ways of being Christian. Though many would probably label them "Conservative" and "Liberal," but that is not a good fit today. Both labels are too extreme and politically influenced today in fact, both could possibly pass for some sort of political religion in themselves.

There is much about the "traditional" way of being Christian. Neither can claim to be the Christian tradition. Both are ways of seeing the traditional. The difference between the "traditional" and the "emerging" of seeing Christianity and being Christian concerns specific conflicts as well as more foundational issues. These include a biblical worldview of God, Jesus, the Holy Spirit, Bible, faith, and the Christian Life. In the contemporary church today specific issues divide for example:

1. Ordination of women – the "traditional" way of being Christian did not ordain women, and in many places still do not today. The "emerging" way does ordain women even to Bishop.

2. Homosexuals and Lesbians – the "traditional" way of Christianity continues to regard any lesbian or homosexual behavior as sinful. The only exceptions for homosexual and lesbian Christians are for celibacy or conversion to heterosexuality. For the question whether sexually active Christian gays and lesbians are not a question today in the "emerging" way or form of Christianity. Also in the "emerging" form of Christianity, gays and lesbians in committed relationships can be married and ordained.

3. Christian exclusivism – Is there only one true religion? Only one path to salvation and heaven? Or are there several true religions, several paths to salvation and heaven? The "traditional" way of being Christian from the beginning and still is confident that Christianity is the one and "only way." Today, the "Emerging" way has changed in many church cultures today. Poll after poll shows that most are responding in the affirmative. That there are more than one way to heaven. The emerging way is willing to corporate with secular culture.

4. The "emerging" Christianity does not affirm the statement, "My religion is the only true religion." Less than one quarter affirmed; and those affirming are in churches that affirm the "traditional" way of Christianity. But three quarters

did not affirm, and this is typical of the "emerging" way of contemporary Christianity.

Both the "traditional" and the "emerging" are present in the churches across this nation today, with deeply divided congregations. As stated earlier, we live in a time of conflict and change in the church.

THE BIBLE AS THE HEART OF EARLIER CHRISTIANITY

The "traditional" Christianity paradigm sees the Bible as sacred, but ultimately centered in the God of the Bible. This is who we are. The "emerging" paradigm sees the Bible as sacred Scripture. But unlike the traditional paradigm, the emerging paradigm sees the Bible's status as the "Holy Bible," but as the result of historical process – not the result of its divine origin. This process is referred to as canonization.

The emerging Christianity paradigm seems to be designed primarily for those people who are no longer satisfied with the traditional version of Christianity which to them no longer works. This new version includes encounters with the modern and postmodern world – including science, historical scholarship, religious pluralism, racism, and cultural diversity.

The emerging Christianity developed over the most recent past and has become a major grass-roots movement within traditional mainline denominations. Sadly, in this crucial time of change and conflict within the church; causing a split; however, there have been several splits within the split. As stated earlier in this book, many people are seeking the authentic Christianity that connects with a deeper biblical worldview in the Christian life:

1. God the Father
2. Christ the Son
3. The Holy Spirit
4. Faith
5. The Bible

6. Biblical authority
7. Atonement
8. Resurrection
9. Believers
10. The Creed
11. Prayer
12. Fasting
13. Christianity

WHAT'S THE NEXT MOVE?

Now that we understand more about the cause of the conflict in the church, it is clear that we need the compelling love of Christ burning like a flame of fire in our hearts for the Word of truth and Spiritually famished world.

Behold, the days come, saith the Lord GOD, "That I will send a famine in the land, not a famine of bread, nor a thirst for water, but of hearing the words of the LORD. (Amos 8:11 KJV)

Amos was describing a special type of famine – a problem with the ears, not the stomach. Amos was warning about a loss of hunger for God and His truth. Notice, this is a self-inflicted famine. Perhaps we are in the beginning days of a "hearing famine" in our generation which will intensify over time. This isn't the only time we find such prophecies in the Word of God.

While many of the churches have no idea what is going on, secularism and postmodernism are working very hard to wipe Christianity from public view. If not countered, soon government overreach will probably come to their aid with some law (stated to be in the best interest of the people) to subtly whack away at our religious freedom and Constitutional rights. All of their actions are happening in the humanistic attempt to destroy or silence the Christian and Christianity's influence without their prior knowledge:

- The prophet Ezekiel says, "Disaster will come upon disaster, and rumor will be upon rumor. Then they will seek a vision from a prophet; but the law will perish from the priest, and counsel from the elders." (Ezekiel 7:26 NKJV)
- The prophet Micah also warmed, "Therefore you shall have night without vision, and you shall have darkness without divination; the sun shall go down on the prophets, and the day shall be dark for them." (Micah 3:6 NKJV)
- Now listen to Paul in the New Testament, he said," But know this, that in the last days perilous times will come: For men will ... always learning and never able to come to the knowledge of the truth." (2 Timothy 3:1,2,7 NKJV)

Certainly it feels like those days are upon us. Look around you. Everywhere you turn, there is widespread *seeing, hearing, and emotional famines, coupled with calamity after calamity, conspiracy theories, and rumors,* perilous times, and all the while learning has accelerated without the ability to come to (or discern) the knowledge of the truth.

People are moving to and fro seeking significance (status) but they have lost their taste for the objective, infallible truth of God's Word.

Jay Leach

The Psalmist cried, "We are given no signs from God; no prophets are left, and none of us knows how long this will be." (Psalm 74:9 NIV)

THE FALLING AWAY

As if the church is not troubled enough, in this section we confront the discouraging news of modern-day "apostacy" for the church, but post modernism's "deconstruction" for this country and Western civilization. Realizing, that this problem is one of the signs of the end times. As we see so many others' lights began to dim, we must take heed to ourselves and remember that He who has begun a good work in us has promised to complete what He started. Praise God! These situations happen so fast and furious today, that something can be happening in the culture world around us which has a profound effect on us – and not being watchful the church will be hit broadside with a situation and people; whose attempt is to destroy it or at least try to give it a black eye.

WILLFUL BLINDNESS

I have observed, as I am sure you have, the power of what I call "willful blindness." That is a dominant promoted by the media and willingly adopted by a critical mass of people who believe a "lie" so badly that they will close their minds to all contrary evidence. When such a cultural movement gains momentum, people stare at facts and filter out what they don't want to believe.

Contrary evidence will be ignored or reinterpreted to fit their deepest wishes. And the more people who believe the lie, the harder it is for those who wish to counter it. In a spirit of euphoria, (the spirit of Babylon is at work here), all warning signs are brushed away. *Then unexpectedly, we realize that we are in a world where facts really do not matter.* But then the mighty effect of suggestive enthusiasm, when the visible success and agreement of hundreds confirm to him or her the rightness of the new doctrine. When they find themselves in a minority in the midst of this zealous majority – such an experience causes the individual to succumb to "the *magical influence* of what we designate as *"willful blindness."* I pray we get the point here!

Ordinary people, simply concerned about living their own lives, can be motivated to become a part of an evil movement, action or act through intimidation, or the herd mentality. Yes, it is possible for ordinary people to commit atrocities they never thought possible when they are swept into a cultural current where everyone is both expected to fall in line and be rewarded for it.

Soon in such a climate, anyone who swims against the stream is demonized by lies, false evidence, and ridicule. With such pressure, even rational and decent people who refuse to cooperate begin to question their own sanity. Can they alone be right when everyone else is wrong?

Another case in point: Often we are faced with a situation that is unfounded. The story is told of a popular young pastor, who wrote a book conveying biblical advice about love and relationships – encouraging young people to make better choices. Note this passage from his book: "The world takes us to a silver screen on which flickering images of passion and romance play, and as we watch, the world says, 'This is love.' God takes us to the foot of a tree on which a naked and bloodied man hangs and says, "This is love."

He had written a bestseller book at age twenty-two; He became very popular with his preaching, writing, and counseling, as well as twenty two years pastoral ministry in a local church. Some years later he announced his marriage had come to an end. Later he disclosed the following:

"I have undergone a massive shift in regard to my faith in Jesus. The secular phrase for this is *"deconstruction[46]."* The biblical phrase is *"falling away."* By all measurements that I have for defining Christians, I am not a Christian. Many people tell me that there is a different way to practice faith and I want to remain open to this, but I'm not there now."

This is ripping me up, because this is happening so expectantly today. So many others seem to be falling away from Christ and His gospel. The song writer said, "Where could I go but to the Lord?" People are believing that such a place exist where they can go without the Lord! This phenomenon is not new. Even as the record shows, the first generation of Christians had to counter this same problem. Paul in writing to the Colossians and to Philemon, sent greetings from his coworker Demas (see Colossians 4:14; Philemon 1:24).

Sadly, in his final letter to Timothy, "Demas has forsaken me, having loved this present world." See (2 Timothy 4:10). Jude, the half-brother of Jesus, the son of Joseph and Mary, wrote desperately

---

[46]   Assessed 12/16/22https//www.Philosophy/basics.com. Deconstruction is a 20th Century school in philosophy. All is theory of literally citizens criticisms the traditional assumptions about certainty, identity, and truth; asserts that words can only refer to other words; and attempts to demonstrate how statements about any test subverts their own meaning.

urging the saints: "To contend earnestly for the faith which was once for all delivered to the saints." (Jude 3)

Certainly, all of us admit the apostles continue to help us today as we face the same problem of those falling away.[47] However the present-day apostasy seems to have suddenly accelerated in our time.

Notice, in all of this, let's keep it real, the central issue here is not that people are falling away from the church or even those falling away from the faith – as important as the both of them are. The chief issue here is their falling away from Jesus Christ, and His gospel. Can you imagine what it takes for the branches to cut themselves off from the vine? This philosophical confusion has been imported into much of the American church. When secular cultural (the world) puts an immoral proposal to the church, many churches compromise "just to get along."

Of how much sorer punishment, suppose ye, shall he be thought worthy, who hath trodden underfoot the Son of God, and hath counted the blood of the covenant, wherewith He was sanctified, and unholy thing, and hath done unto the Spirit of grace?" (Hebrews 10:29 KJV)

Hebrews 10:26-29 contain the *fourth warning passage* of Hebrews (2:1-4). While the surrounding verses (vv. 19-39) contain related exhortations, but the *warning* itself is to these verses. They warn of the critical **danger of turning** from Christ's *once for all*, perfect sacrifice, back to their old ways. **If we sin willfully** reveals that this act is deliberate. This reference here is not to an occasional act of sin *which can be confessed and forgiven*, but to a conscious rejection of God (study carefully 1 John 1;8,9).

The truth is every apostate is an unbeliever, but not every unbeliever is an apostate. There are many people around the world who are unbelievers because they have never had the opportunity to hear the gospel. But an apostate has heard the gospel even professed

---

[47] Falling away and apostasy are the biblical expressions for the secular word "deconstruction."

to be a follower of Christ. But at some point, they **turn their backs on the Savior.**

Their commitment wasn't authentic, and neither was their decision authentic. In reality they are Christians in pretense. Actually, they are non-Christians. Why am I stressing this theme so hard? The average church has apostasy with empty pews no matter rather they were ever filled in the first place. Deconstruction, relativism, secularism, and all of their cousins have come against the church. But this is really a prophecy about tomorrow with implications for us today. We know from our study of prophecy that this is a sudden event without any sign. Both the rapture and the falling away can happen at any moment. What is the point for the alarm and concern?

Rather than coming to Christ in droves, people are convinced that there is another way to heaven, or it just doesn't matter. Although we see the acceleration of all events of prophecy. The falling away is a predictive sign of the last days. I say again, the core or center issue is not that people are falling away from the church or even falling away from the faith. We are talking about falling away from Jesus Christ, Himself! The Greek word for apostasy is found in the New Testament (see Acts 21:21; II Thess. 2:3). Again, the word means "a falling away from:"

- A deserting or turning from a position or view formally held.
- Spiritual apostasy happens when a person who once claimed to be a believer, departs from what he or she formerly professed to believe.
- An apostate is not one who was saved and then lost their salvation.
- An apostate, having claimed to be a believer, never was saved in the beginning.

I repeat every apostate is an unbeliever, but not every unbeliever is an apostate.

CHRIST'S SECOND COMING

After Paul finished writing I Thessalonians, he received word that the believers in Thessalonica were being misled by false teachers who were confusing the believers with erroneous ideas about the Second Coming. In every generation, Christians must face the dilemma of how to live in the tension between His First Coming and His possible "imminent" return [in the air] for His Church and the impossibility of predicting when that moment will arrive. Many Christians unfortunately settle the problem by:

- *Living* as if Christ will not return.
- Departing for other religions that have no Savior nor responsibilities.
- Believing false teachers, secularism, paganism and other natural religions.
- People are being moved by the doctrines of demons, which are gaining members and *political* strength daily as the world grows darker.
- Sadly, many who are dropping out today join a group called "nones." This group claims to be non-affiliated with any religion or belief system.

Why am I repeating myself in this section? Because the apostasy is important, often overlooked, it is on the rise; as it is another sign of the end; which is hurtling toward us with ever increasing speed. This falling away that Paul was writing about is not just some gradual defection from Christ. Paul called it the "falling away." As we speak though it is one of the important doctrines of the hour, but it be listed among the silent issues in many churches. Another sign of the imminent return of Christ is a rising number of self-styled Christians who ultimately *reject Christ*. Mark this last statement!

The Bible says, "Now brethren, concerning the coming of our Lord Jesus Christ and our gathering together to Him, we ask you, not to be soon shaken in mind or troubled, either by spirit or by word or by letter, as if from us, as though the day of Christ had come. Let no one deceive you by any means; *for the Day of the Lord will not come unless the falling away comes first,* and the man of sin is revealed, the son of perdition." (2 Thessalonians 2:1-3 NKJV) Emphasis added. That is a predictive sign of the approach of Christ return – a great falling away will happen.

STAY IN SHAPE (SPIRITUAL EXERCISE)

If a baseball player, basketball player, and a boxer are so concerned about taking care of their bodies – as evidenced by the great expense they give up for it; shouldn't we be just as dedicated to taking care of our *souls?* The Bible says,

"For bodily exercise profits a little, but godliness is profitable for all things, having promise of the life that now is and of that which is to come." (1 Timothy 4:8 NKJV)

THERE IS HOPE

Like a pool of stagnant water, when our faith is gone for whatever reason, we too are useless and stagnant. It breaks my heart; that our people are falling away from Christ and His gospel in droves. One conduit feeding this phenomenon is the lack of spiritual and biblical knowledge coupled with the lack of corresponding practical experience with guidance.

But don't despair all is not lose. There is hope even in the face of apostasy and desertion of Christians from the church. God knows those who are in His true body worldwide, and He will protect them and bring them home. Jesus said,

"I give them eternal life, and they shall never perish; neither shall anyone snatch them out of My hand. My Father, who has given them to Me, is greater than all; and no one is able to snatch them out of My Father's hand." (John 10:28-29 NKJV)

The apostle Paul passed along the same hope, when he declared, "He who has begun a good work in you will complete it until the day of Jesus Christ." (Philippians 1:6 NKJV)

Jude the half-brother of Jesus, concludes his book of exuberant praise to "Him who is able to keep you from stumbling, and present you faultless before the presence of His glory with exceeding joy." (see Jude 24 NKJV)

Praise be to the Lord, who alone is able to keep you from being deceived. Note, Jude does not use the word falling but stumbling. Only a person who is already walking or running can stumble. God is able to keep us from stumbling. Wouldn't it be wonderful to see a great spiritual revival before the church is raptured?

Only a person who is already running or walking can stumble!

SERVING SELF

According to Paul, in 2 Timothy 3, the days before the tribulation will be perilous because people will love only themselves. They will be "boasters, proud, blasphemers" (v.2). Then in v. 13: *"But evil men and imposters will grow worse and worse, deceiving and being deceived."*(NKJV)

"Worse and worse!" With these three words, Paul predicted people will descend into accelerating godlessness as we approach the tribulation. It is important to note, Paul's focus was not on bad times, but on bad people. As John Calvin wrote, "The hardness or danger of this time is in Paul's view to be, not war, famine or diseases, nor any other calamities or ills that befall the body – but the wicked and depraved ways of men."[48]

Paul gave us nineteen specific character traits of what people will be like. In other words, nineteen expressions to depict the nature of godlessness in the last days (see 2 Timothy 3). His words move from selfish people to splintered families, to shattered societies. As stated earlier, these people love to talk about themselves – building themselves up. They want everyone else to love them as much as they love themselves. They are proud and haughty people, which means

---

[48] John Calvin, *The Second Epistle of Paul the Apostle to the Corinthians and the Epistles to Timothy, Titus and Philemon* (Grand Rapids, MI: W. B. Eerdmans Publishing Company, 1996), 322.

they have no regard for others. They are intent on pushing others out of the way so they can stand taller. There are five descriptive words that depict the brokenness these people cause in their own families in the last days. People will be:

1. Disobedient to parents
2. Unthankful
3. Unholy
4. Unloving
5. Unforgiving

REVEAL THE DARKNESS

One day I turned over a board laying on the ground, as I looked down bugs, ants, worms, and other critters were scampering for other darkened hideaways. They obviously preferred the darkness over the light. They love darkness. Since we have this wonderful partnership with God, how could we ever become partners with that which belongs to sin and darkness? "What communion has light with darkness?" (2 Corinthians 6:14 (NKJV). We are children of light and ought to walk in the light. Darkness produces sin and lies – the fruit of the light is goodness, righteousness, and truth. The light cannot compromise with the darkness; *it can only expose it.* (see John 3:19-21 and 1 John 5-10)

In Ephesians 5:11-14, Paul tells us something else: *"And have no fellowship with the unfruitful works of darkness, but rather expose them. For it is shameful even to speak of those things which are done by them in secret. But all things that are exposed are made manifest by the light, for whatever makes manifest is light.* Therefore he continues: *'Awake, you who sleep, arise from the dead, and Christ will give you light.'"* (NKJV)

Remember that board I turned over earlier, the bugs and other critters fled seeking a dark place, like under the board. They prefer the darkness – and the light expels them. In the same manner, the world may be offended when we walk in the light and seek, through our life living to reveal the holiness of Christ. My vision through the years has been to encourage people to experience the power of the Spirit.

I sound the alarm through this book and the other books that I've written and published, in addition to the thousands of lectures and manuscripts I've been blessed to present, always warning about the anti-Christian forces trying to cancel true Christianity and religious freedoms, by smothering the biblical perspective, and world view from our national life. Standing strong for biblical truth is only possible if we are empowered by the Holy Spirit. Sadly, it seems that too many of our pastors and other Christians, don't realize what's hitting them. I pray my books and media ministry will help provide answers. I believe this is the most important book I've written. We must boldly raise our voices to push back against the cancel culture before it's too late – we owe it to generations Y and Z.

Managing Expectations

As various people join our churches from different generations; they will no doubt bring different expectations. Youngsters entering the church today have had a life almost totally unto themselves, interfacing on social media with peers rather than mentors. I read a story about a man rushing to drop off his 19 year old daughter, who was running late for work. Meantime to save time he handed her several letters along with stamps and return address labels to put together as they rode along.

He looked up in the rearview mirror, to find his daughter searching for a YouTube video on how to mail a letter. She had no idea where the stamp went because she'd never mailed a physical letter before. Undoubtedly, she had paid no attention to where stamps go on envelops, even though letters are sent and received at their home daily.

The father exclaimed that he didn't know how he should feel after seeing this situation; should he feel disappointed or should he feel outdated. Sometimes younger generations have unique experiences, they bring to the church. Often they bring unique expectations with them to the church meeting. Additionally, they may bring unique expectations with them. Then sometimes their innovative ideas can shake the church, especially when they are asking questions such as how to change to terms for service for church officers rather than, like the deacons are there for life in some churches.

Sometimes they just drop the bomb of what they are feeling or thinking, causing some heartburn for the old guard. Sometimes things are ignored, with the thought it will go away. I believe we can begin to build a bridge between our differences by understanding preferences, sometimes a task has to completed so the boomer may prefer the task done in a manner they have used in the past, but the Millennials or Gen Zers want to approach the task in a new way. This could mean unnecessary trouble – earlier I spoke about winning an argument but losing a relationship. Why do I want to win this? What am I to gain? What will it cost me and what am I willing to sacrifice. Another consideration is "if it isn't broke don't fix it."

STUDY GUIDE: WORKSHEET AND REFLECTIONS
CHAPTER 12

1. Define the "apostasy" the apostle Paul spoke of?

2. The Day of the Lord will not come unless the _____ _____ first.

3. God knows those who are _____ and He will _____ them and bring _____.

4. Without the _____ of the _____ _____ we are not effective at countering cancel culture.

5. The light cannot _____ with the darkness, it can only _____ it.

6. What communion does light have with darkness: _____?

7. The world may be _____ when we _____ in the _____.

Chapter Thirteen

NONE BUT THE RIGHTEOUS

*"He made Him who knew no sin to be sin for us,
that we might become the righteousness of God
in Him"* (2 Corinthians 5:21 NKJV).

*"Do not be conformed to this world, but be transformed
by the renewal of your mind, that by testing you may
discern what is the will of God, what is good and
acceptable and perfect"* (Romans 12:2 ESV).

Many Christians sense that things are not right in this country. During my 26.5-year Army career I returned home from overseas tours five times. Each time I returned to a noticeably different and far less Christian America. Yet, from what I saw in other lands America the Beautiful was still the best place in the world to come home to. I loved this country then and I love it today. I teach in and pastor the Bread of life Christian Center and Church, our greatest mission over the past 25 years has been to make disciples, who make disciples. Everywhere you turn people are crying, "it's just awful!"

Sadly, many Christians individually or corporately are not equipped for what is happening. Therefore, we should be in a right relationship with God and return to the basics of a biblical worldview, in order to respond to the new (for us) situations we are facing today. Without such basic analysis, believers may even embrace segments of what they do not realize is very unbiblical. The Pope told the world on the newscast on January 25, 2023, that homosexuality is sin, but not a crime. Biblically analyze that statement.

THE PROBLEM IS NOT NEW

In Psalm 11, King David grieved over the troubles caused by religious and cultural destruction from within. He passionately expresses himself in a question that has been echoed down through the centuries of the church: *"If the foundations are destroyed, what can the righteous do?"* (Psalm 11:3 ESV). When, like, David, Christians see that, *"the wicked bend the bow; they have their arrow to the string to shoot in the dark **at the upright in heart"** (Psalm 11:2 ESV).*

More than likely, they will follow the crooked advice offered by David's enemies: *"Flee like a bird to your mountain"* (Psalm 11:1 ESV). Some Christians have acted on this temptation, creating stockpiled closed communities. However, we cannot quite. Though the foundations of America and Western civilization *are shaken,* so many have accepted *the new worldview,* we have undying hope for there is one foundation that lasts.

There is one sure place of refuge, God! He made the mountains and will one day remake His creation into a truly new and renewed world where **righteousness** dwells. And we know, with our eyes of faith – that clothed with His righteousness we shall *"behold His face"* (v. 7).

WHAT MUST THE RIGHTEOUS DO?

Righteous people do righteous deeds, but righteous deeds do not make people righteous. There is only one way to righteousness and that is through faith in Christ's finished work. The apostle Paul referenced this reality in revealing that the tragedy of the Jewish people was that they were going about trying to establish their own righteousness based on keeping the Law. Knowing that our Father is testing and refining us even when the foundations are crumbling and falling apart, we seek to display righteousness to a watching world.

We are "out of Babylon" (the world of darkness) and clearly, we can't give up or give in! Realizing, that is the constant temptation when things get tough. So, now faced with unprecedented opposition to truth, and the Christian faith – a faith once delivered to the saints (see Jude 3) we must stand boldly! This is a time when the response of the righteous is crucial for the very survival of the gospel in our day. We can reign in life by receiving this great gift of righteousness and knowing that we have been made righteous by faith (because we believe, not because we act right).

I pray the present-day church will discern the *true* nature of this situation and react in a manner that honors Christ and His gospel, as the early church did. Conforming with the world as we described above is the very *worse response possible:*

- The Apostle Peter warned those of the Dispersion .... "As obedient children do not be conformed to the passion of your former ignorance" (1 Peter 1:1, 14 ESV).
- Paul repeats the warning to Christians living in wicked Nero's Rome. "Do not be conformed to this world" (Romans 12:2 ESV).

In the pagan society and regime under which Christians lived in the first century,

- They were <u>constantly tempted to modify their beliefs and adapt their behavior to a culture that did not share their essential faith.</u>
- Throughout history Christians have been in similar social situations, in cultures and under governments <u>that had no regard for Christian principles.</u>

Christians, not just in America, but everywhere, are called by God in His Word:

- To *know* the particular ideas that constitute the world's view, or pattern of thinking and belief.
- Then, we can both resist the *Big Lie* and make a statement of the *Truth* that understands and exposes the Lie and offers the only true hope of the gospel.
- Ignorance in this matter only produces faith-destroying conformity and compromise.

FEARING THE CULTURE

Today, Christians often conform or compromise out of *fear*. We may fear verbal abuse, politics, accusations of hate speech, loss of friends, job, respect, or physical abuse. It is increasingly difficult for Christian groups to sponsor events. In light of all the above, how can Christians speak the gospel truth in the public square? Today many operate under the radar, which to many seem to be the only alternative. The temptation is for Christians to shutter the windows, lock all doors and disappear from sight, or contribute to the community *through culturally approved acts* of service. Service is certainly great but notice, with each of these alternatives the Word of Truth is silenced! It is obvious, that if we are going to be *sentinels* for the kingdom:

1. We must consider that today's situations require integrity, wisdom from above, and grace for the ministries as well as for all Christians.
2. We must pray fervently for one another, especially for striving Christian millennials and Gen Zers also for those who come after them.

CULTURAL AGREEMENT

Many modern Christians believe that the churches problems getting along with the culture are mainly self-imposed and – to them avoidable:

- The culture actually hates us because to them we are socially obnoxious and our approach to evangelism is definitely all wrong.
- Others believe that the culture's opposition will disappear if the church tweaks its witness strategies, update its message, and participates more compassionately for the earth and its inhabitants.
- The purpose for church is to win *souls* for Christ! Yet, to others, it has become the promotion of this-worldly "human progression" as defined by the surrounding culture.

Many pastors and other church leaders tend to agree with that negative view of the church. While we can always find weaknesses in the church and its faith and practices, many in leadership deny that this present generation is different than any prior generation. So, it's business as usual (seeing no need for change – drive on!). This attitude fuels the perception that the world is upcoming, "unglued" and concludes that Christianity has failed.

Rather than seeking a coherent biblical strategy of the true Christian faith and biblical worldview, however, they attempt to figure out what aspects of Christian values that the world might like – social justice, tolerance for differing views of truth, forms of mysticism and then prioritize these things as the heart of the gospel. Certainly, the rationale behind this required need for change is the known fact the current generations do not find it immediately to their liking or taste. As Christ's watchmen in our present-day situation, to be liked must never be our priority over true faithfulness to the Gospel. Otherwise, compromise is obvious and could seem like the virtuous way to go, but the results are serious sinful disobedience. A major threat to true Christianity comes from some of the highly polished conferences where cultural leaders of many non-Christian persuasions are invited to lecture. It may seem to be the answer to the churches' problem. However, a clear biblical undergirding of its convictions and commitments in many are not a requirement. Some churches have been totally destroyed spiritually, while others are disrupted over politics and other issues. They also invite people with highly controversial views on the Bible, gender, and sexuality.

The church has been guilty of all sorts of sins. But these deep results of inquiry into the contemporary church's faith and practices does not come from within its great tradition of prophetic calls of repentance and return to the "old paths," but from without, from the premise of a biblically hostile worldview that Christians cannot possibly hope to appease while remaining true and faithful to Christ and His body, the church.

So many Christians have made the mistake of believing that the surrounding culture is redemptive work of the Spirit that shares authority with the Scriptures. For example, Emergent church leader Kester Brewin, believes the church must admit "our dependence on our host culture"[49] and "open ourselves to …. and become adopted to it,"[50] recognizing its essential goodness."[51] Acceptance of Brewin's analysis, conforming to culture seems like the natural thing to do. However, the foundations for church and that of the culture are not the same. The Scripture is clear:

Do not be unequally yoked together with unbelievers. For what fellowship has righteousness with lawlessness? And what communion has light with darkness? And what accord has Christ with Belial? Or what part has a believer with an unbeliever? And what agreement has the temple of God with idols. For you are the temple of the living God. As God has said:

"I will dwell in them and walk among them.
I will be their God and they shall be My people."
Therefore, "Come out from among them
And be separate, says the Lord.
Do not touch what is unclean,
And I will receive you."
"I will be a Father to you,

---

[49]   Kester Brewin, *Signs of Emergence: A vision for Church that is Organic/ Networked/ Bottom Decentralized / bottom-up/ communal/ Flexible/ Always Evolving* (Grand Rapids, Baker, 2007), 53.

[50]   Brewin, *Signs of Emergence,* 104.

[51]   Brewin, *Signs of Emergence,* 128.

And you shall be My sons and daughters,
Says the LORD Almighty." 2 Cor. 6:14-18 NKJV

The Apostle Paul goes on to exhort Christians everywhere, *"Therefore, having these promises, beloved, let us cleanse ourselves from all filthiness of the flesh and of the spirit, perfecting holiness in the fear of God"* (2 Cor. 7:1 NKJV).

They were to wash away all dirt from both flesh and spirit, meaning those actions and attitudes that were the results having false teachers in their midst (see 6:14). The point of cleansing is perfecting holiness. That is, bringing holiness to completion in the fear of God. One thing is sure, the culture has a mind of its own, a worldview, the wisdom of this world," which is the Lie that makes people worship the creature, rather than the Creator.

There is so much more at stake since the contemporary Christians conform to the culture – as they compromise with the culture's religious convictions and depart from the faith and biblical witness. Certainly, the world does not need more conformity; it needs to be transformed. They need to hear the Word from God, from outside of itself. They need to hear and see Truth.

STUDY GUIDE: WORKSHEET AND REFLECTIONS
CHAPTER 13

1. In Psalm 11, King David grieved over the troubles caused by
    _____ and _____ destruction from within.

2. In such cases, more than likely they will follow the crooked
    advice offered by _____ _____: *"Flee like a bird
    to your mountain."* (Psalm 11:2 ESV).

3. Some _____ have acted on this temptation (to
    flee) creating *closed* communities stockpiled _____
    _____. Others who don't go that far are still
    _____ to _____ (v.1).

4. As the foundations of this country are shaken, so have
    accepted the _____ Worldview.

5. There is one sure place of refuge, _____
    (v.7).

6. In the pagan society and regime Christians lived in the 1st
    Century, they were constantly tempted to _____
    their _____ and _____ their behavior to a
    culture that did not share their essential faith.

7. The purpose for the church is win souls for Christ.
    Yet, to _____, it has become the promotion of
    this worldly "human progression" as defined by the
    _____ _____.

Chapter Fourteen

THE APOSTOLIC WAY

"It is written, man shall not live by bread alone, but by every word that proceedeth out of the mouth of God" (Matthew 4:4 KJV).

Christianity in the United States has lost the confidence of so many Christians that they are now saying "post Christianity" much like their secular counterparts. They observe:

- They observe the numerical decline and declining morale of the "mainline" churches.
- They observe many people trusting science and reason, or other disciplines, others are turning to conferences and seminars, still others turn to trying religions and cults to meet their needs.
- They observe many people living as if there is no God.
- They observe the successful invasion and entrenchment from the wide assumption that all religions are "the same."
- They observe the widespread growth of secularism and post modernism.

From such observations, Christianity's future looks dimmer, than a star-bright contagious movement. Not only that, when they see unanointed denominational leaders more concerned with political correctness, and hierarchical advancement, than with any concern for the unsaved or spread of the gospel of Jesus Christ.

Many of us have learned over time that the future of Christianity is modeled in pioneering local churches. Moreover, we are learning to view our world through two lenses "Secularity"[52] and "Modernity[53]" – which provide important means to understanding our opportunity in this present era, no matter what it looks like. We touched on these two views in earlier section, but now we will go to a deeper discussion.

SECULARITY

Secularization is defined as the withdrawal of the church's influence, in whole areas of life and thought. This menace has advanced for the past five hundred years and continues to this day unchecked.[54] Consequently, we observe an astoundingly increasing population of "secular people"[55] who maneuver their whole lives without profound influence of any Christian church whatsoever. Older folk use to say, "that's cut and dry," in other words the entire world or community at least marched to the rules set by the church, during that time the church played a significant role in developing a worldview that influenced practically everybody in this country.

Today, however, a great percentage of Americans are secular and our society's subcultures march to a number of competing views. In

---

[52] Secularity, secular, and secularism is the state of being unrelated or neutral in regard to religion or irreligion. Denotes attitudes, activities, or other things that have no religious or spiritual basis. Microsoft Bing (dictionary) – assessed 6/11/22.

[53] Modernity, A topic of humanities and social sciences is both a historical period and the ensemble of particular socio-culture norms, attitudes, and practices in the Renaissance period. A condition of social existence that is radically different to all past forms of human existence. The quality or condition of being modern.

[54] George G. Hunter III. *How to Reach Secular People* (Nashville: Abingdon Press, 1992) Chapters 1-2

[55] Ibid. page 59

this more secular country, an increasing number of people live their whole lives without the influence of Christianity or the church.

In fact, it is not strange to meet people on a daily basis who have never physically been inside a church building for any reason. Many express that they have no need nor desire to change that status. The situation has become critical, due to the growing secularism, atheism, an influx of religions, cults, and beliefs due to multiculturalism.

MODERNITY

Through the synergism of many historical events the Western world became not only "secular," but also "modern" – from the impact of the eighteenth-century "Enlightenment," also known as the "Age of Reason."[56] The Enlightenment came into Eighteenth-century Europe with gigantic confidence *in human reason*. It produced the intellectual foundations for Western society for the next two centuries. The Enlightenment's teachings are more widely believed by more Western people than are the teachings of Christianity. Below is a summarization of eight of the teachings that have been instrumental in shaping the worldview of the Western world:

1. The Enlightenment taught that human beings are basically rational. What separates human beings from the beasts of the field, forests, and jungles is not creation in God's image but their capacity for reasonable thought.

2. The Enlightenment taught that; human beings are basically good. In a challenge to Christian doctrine of original sin, the Enlightenment was confident of humanity's essential goodness. Enlightenment leaders observed, of course, that people do not always behave in good or reasonable ways. They attributed this to the *unjust* or *oppressive environment* in which people live. Fix the system, and the rationality and

---

[56] The Enlightenment was an intellectual and cultural movement in the 18th century that emphasized reason over superstition, and science over blind faith. Merriam-Webster.com//dictionary.

goodness of people surface – a half-truth that has been with us ever since.

3. Following Isaac Newton's discovery of gravity and the development of his orderly, predictable, machinelike, closed-system model of the universe, many Western people no longer expected [or they had trouble perceiving] miracles; the supernatural became optional, and God was uninvolved. This is called Deism.

4. Enlightenment leaders taught that people could base morality on reason alone, without the aid of revelation or religion.

5. Enlightenment leaders taught that we could build and manage cities and societies on reason alone, without reference to revealed values or church leadership.

6. The movement was confident that science and education would liberate humanity from its entrenched problems like poverty, crime, injustice, and war.

7. The enlightenment spread the confidence that all problems are solvable, and therefore progress is "inevitable."

8. The Enlightenment's philosophy of "natural religion" taught that all religions are essentially the same. While Christianity, Hinduism, Buddhism, and Islam, for example, look quite different from one another on the surface, the deeper you go in each, the more similar they become – because all religions are rooted in a common religious consciousness in the human heart.

Today we are faced with unprecedented opposition to the Christian faith – the "faith once delivered to the saints" (see Jude 3). A faith which was once the dominant source of social and moral definitions in Western culture. I think much of the church don't know what time it is, and just how crucial our positive and active response is for the very survival of the gospel today. I pray that in looking back to the history of the church, when religious paganism ruled the culture – that the present-day church will see the true nature of the crisis (beast) and react responsibly in a manner that pleases Christ and His gospel, as the early church did.

All Christians the world over are called by God in His Word to know the particular ideas that make up the world's pattern of thinking and belief; then we can both prayerfully resist the Lie and make a statement of the Truth that exposes the Lie and offer the only true hope in the Gospel.

WHAT MUST THE RIGHTEOUS DO?

Ignorance of the answer will produce faith-destroying conformity, compromise, and the Word of Truth will be silenced. The question arises "What must the righteous do?" Certainly, the new situation calls for wisdom and grace for all Christians. We must pray for one another, especially for the Millennials and Gen Zers and those who are coming to pick up the Blood-stained banner after them (see 2 Thessalonians 3:2; 1Corinthians 16:9).

Let us look to the example of the Apostle Paul's prayer request as he sat in a Roman jail chained to an armed soldier. Pray for the prosperity of the Gospel of Christ – and pray for the Word of God and pray for the safetv y of God's men and women, who preach and teach it around the world for "there are many adversaries." (1 Corinthians 16:9 NKJV)

[Pray] also for me, that words may be given to me in opening my mouth boldly to proclaim the mystery of the gospel, for which I am an ambassador in chains, that I may declare it boldly, as I ought to speak," (Ephesians 6:19-20 ESV)

The Word of God and prayer are two resources God has given to the church to overcome the enemy and gain territory for the glory of God:

So now, brethren, I commend you to God and to the word of His grace, which is able to build you up and give an inheritance among all those who are sanctified. (Acts 20:32 NKJV)

But we will give ourselves continually to prayer and to the ministry of the Word. (Acts 6:4 NKJV)

Additionally, as Christians we are told to also:

- Watch and pray for opportunities to serve Christ (see Colossians 4:2).
- We should not pray for ourselves only, but we should also pray for fellow Christians (v. 3).

Paul was never too proud to ask for prayer. He desired the power to be able to share the mystery (see 3:1-12), the very message that had brought him to jail. "Ambassador in bonds" is a unique title, yet that is exactly what Paul was. Chained to a different soldier every six hours gave Paul tremendous opportunity to witness for Christ.

Paul closes this epistle knowing that his friends would want to know his condition and needs. But Paul was a true saint, desiring to give his friends comfort too as he drew from God's supply for his every need.

STUDY GUIDE: WORKSHEET AND REFLECTIONS
CHAPTER 14

1. Christianity in the United States has lost the confidence of so many Christians that they are now saying "_____ _____" much like their secular counterparts.

2. Look back at the text and list several reasons why the Christian voice is coming to such conclusions: 1) _____ 2) _____ 3. _____.

3. _____ is defined as the withdrawal of the church's presence.

4. The survival of the gospel of Jesus Christ is more threatened today, perhaps than any other time since the 1st Century. Paganism ruled the culture in that day. Paganism is on the march in this country. What must the righteous do especially for Gen Zers? Review the lesson text and write a comment below:

5. The Word of God and prayer are two resources God has given to the church to _____ _____ _____ and gain territory for the _____ _____.

6. As Christians, we are also to _____ and _____ for opportunities to serve Christ (see Colossians 4:2)

7. Pray for the prosperity of the gospel of Christ and pray for the safety of God's workman for "there are many adversaries." (1 Corinthians 16:9 NKJV)

Chapter Fifteen

YOUR SPIRITUAL WARFARE

"Finally, be strong in the Lord and in the strength of His might. Put on the whole armor of God, that you may be able to stand against the schemes of the devil. For we do not wrestle against flesh and blood, but against the rulers, against the authorities, against the cosmic powers over the present darkness, against the spiritual forces of evil in the heavenly places." (Ephesians 6:10-12 ESV)

Today few people in our culture witness open and obvious demonic activity, but demon activity has greatly increased openly and behind the scenes depending on your locale. Even among Christians there is a tendency to discount the demons' influence. Knowing this, Paul taught his followers and also left a *legacy* for future generations – enabling us to recognize and counter demons.

Recognition begins with our understanding that actual spiritual warfare takes place within the hearts and lives of individuals.

Satan's strategies are designed to cripple or disable believers making them miserable and ineffective. Constantly on the move, demons are always looking for an open door through which they can enter to oppress and weaken believers. Therefore, there are no doubt areas in every Christian's life where demonic harassment and oppression are robbing them of the freedom intended for them to have in Christ.

In any warfare it is essential to know your enemy. Therefore, it is necessary to put emphasis on spiritual warfare, as it causes us to become familiar with our enemy, the devil, and how he operates. Understanding the enemy and his mode of operation – enables us to counter his attacks against us. This is why Paul told the Corinthians concerning the devil. "... *We are not ignorant of his devices.*" (2 Corinthians 2:11 KJV)

Beware, an overemphasis on spiritual warfare has the potential to easily have a very poor effect on the Church. Unless spiritual warfare is taught properly, it can be devastating. If this subject is not taught and practiced right, then failure of success could have the people magnifying the devil's power to a higher degree than it deserves.

Such novices will soon convince themselves that Satan is behind everything that occurs, then they become incapable of functioning normally in any capacity in life. In this way the enemy can render them useless to the Kingdom of God. Unfortunately, this has been the outcome with too many people concerning the issue of spiritual warfare in the past. We are commanded in the Scripture to deal with the unseen, invisible forces that Satan has brought against us:

1. "Cast out devils." (see Mark 16:17)
2. "Pull down the strongholds of the mind." (see 2 Corinthians 10:3-5)

This is a part of our Christian duty and responsibility toward the lost, the oppressed, and the demonized. In our own Bread of Life, ministry wide we have to deal with demonic manifestations on occasion. There are millions of people in the world today who are held hostage by the devil *in their minds.* In the gospels we can see how hostile demons are to human beings.

Today, demons are responsible for many *mental* and *physical ailments,* from vicious madness to blindness. When Paul wrote in Ephesians that *"our struggle is not against flesh and blood, but against* the *rulers,* against the *authorities,* against the *powers* <u>of this</u> <u>dark world and against the *spiritual forces* of evil in the heavenly</u> <u>realms."</u> (see Ephesians 6:12 NKJV)

JESUS CAME FOR THIS PURPOSE

First John 3:8 says, "… for this purpose the Son of God was manifested, that He might destroy the works of Satan." The word "destroy" comes from the Greek word *Luo,* and it refers to *the act of untying or unloosing something.* It is the exact word we would use to picture a man who is untying his shoes. In fact, the word *Luo* is used in this exact way in Luke 3:16 KJV, when John the Baptist says, "… But one mightier than I cometh, the latchet of whose shoes I am not worthy to unloose…" Thus, Jesus Christ came into the world to *untie* and *unloose* Satan's binding over us.

At the Cross, Jesus untied Satan's power until His redemptive work was finally completed. *"How God anointed Jesus of Nazareth with the Holy Spirit and with power, who went about doing good and healing all who were oppressed by the devil, for God was with Him."* (Acts 10:38 NKJV)

Without a doubt, in the two verses above, that setting people free from Satan's power is a primary goal of Jesus Christ. Since this is Jesus' primary goal – is there any question about what our primary goal should be as well? In the main time, Satan as the prince of this world is busy influencing and swaying all levels of the leadership of whole countries (i.e. Russia today), families, cultures, societies by planting strongholds of deception in some area of the individual's mind, <u>for the mind is the primary area Satan seeks to attack.</u> If Satan is successful, coupled with his legions of demons he can <u>control and manipulate</u> the individual, and much, much more from that lofty position, remember, he is the prince of this world.

WATCH OUT AMERICA!

The *postmodern secular* culture in America today is driven by whatever can bring our bodies the most pleasure. What can we eat, touch, watch, do, listen to, or engage in to satisfy the *cravings of our bodies?* One writer said, we are swimming in a cultural ocean that cries out with every wave, "Gratify your body!"

This would require a new expression for Christianity as we know it – for the true kingdom of God, Christ, the Holy Spirit (three in One) as when heaven invaded this earth two thousand years ago. As born from above Christians through the "blood of Jesus, the Word of God in tandem with the Holy Spirit, we know where all of this is going.

A secular religion would be required to accommodate such a travesty. It is like upgrading the old skull and cross bones on yesteryears "rat poison" by simply putting a new label on the outside of the container. It kills just the same as the old – because it is the same old "poison." It seems we have a stalemate between two extremes (ultra-Liberalism and ultra-Conservatism) both "isms" are "voluntarily" satanically blind to the fact that each are on a course; which if not corrected will destroy this nation (the United States of America). If not careful – done without a shot fired!

America, having chosen "science" and "reason"[57] over God and Christ has its limitations because it is natural, so the best it can produce is naturalism (just another "ism"), really putting a new label on old secular humanism." It is called civil religion, with the idea of getting rid of God and the things of God, mainly His influence from all aspects of America's life so that the devilish "self" can rule and reign.

But we know that our bodies were not ultimately created for self-gratification – but for God-glorification. In I Corinthians we are told: the body is meant *"for the Lord and the Lord for the body."* God is devoted to our bodies, and He wants you to experience the maximum joy for which your body is built. And further, as the Creator, He knows what will bring them the most pleasure. He has designed our bodies for His glory – and our good.

---

[57]   Assessed 9/27/22 https// Wikipedia.org Reason is the capacity of conscientiously applying logic by drawing conclusions from new or existing information with the aim of finding truth.

HEAR WHAT THE SPIRIT IS SAYING

Obviously, the Spirit is speaking a strong message to us today concerning spiritual warfare. Christian leaders all across this country are awakening to this reality. Church, we must give the Spirit our full attention (heed) to what He is saying to the Church – then proceed with Spirit, the Blood, and the Word of God working in tandem as our guide and foundation.

Basically, Satan influences cultures so that they appeal to the sinfulness of human beings. By shaping a culture's values in this manner, Satan is able to direct human desires and efforts away from God and toward the temporal and meaninglessness.

John says,

"The world is passing away, and the lusts of it; but he who does the will of God abides forever." (I John 2:17 NKJV)

Here John illuminates the brevity of life. To be consumed with this life is to be unprepared for the next. What a sad commentary to invest our resources in what will not last. He views the rise of those who deny the truth of Christ from within the church as an indication of the *beginning of the end of all things* (see v. 18).

At the same time, we gather clearly from the epistles that demons pay attention to individuals, and especially believers. This important truth is particularly presented in discussions today about transgender identity. It is become a cultural norm for males to wish they were females, and females want to be males.

I can't perceive why knowing the truth, men, women, and even children in our culture question whether God's design for their bodies as male and female is a mistake? Contrary to cultural beliefs or desires, the Bible equates our gender identity with our sexual identity and asserts that the way God has made each of us as a man or a woman is good.

I do not pretend to know the depth of the physical, emotional, relational, and other factors behind these desires, but in spite of what educators are spewing out; we do know that God is for our bodies. This is why in His love; He gives us boundaries for our bodies: He loves us and knows what is best for us. These simple truths clarify what we are doing when we ignore God's instructions. Throughout the whole Bible, He gives us boundaries for how our bodies are to be used. The devil opposes all that God does for the good of mankind.

DEMONIC INFLUENCE

He has deployed his demons, his children, his false prophets, and false teachers against God's people in the world today. The Scripture speaks of their use of false doctrine, lies, and deception in the last days. What demons do is *influence* us. They tempt us, twist our thinking and cloud our understanding:

- They lie to us about our identity in Christ
- They are constantly telling us that we are useless and hopeless
- They encourage bitterness and anger
- They destroy healthy relationships
- They stimulate your fears causing us to panic
- They drown you in despair and depression
- They tell you; you can't risk stepping out in faith
- They tell us we are too weak to respond to God's Word
- They push you toward addictions that ruin our lives
- They sometimes ruin your health
- They rob you of your joy

Through these ways demons oppress believers – this gives Paul reason to use this letter to lay out God's defense against demons. Please note in none of the above did Paul mention demon *possession*. In fact the word *possessed* is not found in the gospels. The Greek word is *daimonizomi,* which simply means "demonized." Again demons influence believers – not possess the temple. Satan already knows he can't take away your salvation. But he will try to take away your joy of salvation. Nehemiah 8:10 tells us "the joy of the Lord is my strength." ESV Conversely, losing that joy depletes your spiritual strength. This satanic strategy can be countered by anchoring yourself *unconditionally* on the Word of God, believing *every word* on *every word*.

SATAN'S END TIME OFFENSIVE

Satan will continue to use these tactics against Christians not only in the present age but also in the end times, during the tribulation period. He will be busy throwing flaming darts of depression, doubts, worry, anger, and robbing believers of joy.

OUR GREATER DEFENSE

We know that "Greater is He that is in us than he that is in the world"(see I John 4:4). God has supplied a way out for those who are His. He has given us His indwelling Holy Spirit to help us (see John 14:16). Certainly, this cannot be successful in this warfare in our own human strength (flesh). Please notice Paul's directive to the Ephesians and believers today,

*"Finally, my brethren, be strong in the Lord and in the power of His might. Put on the whole armor of God, that you may be able to stand against the wiles of the devil. For we do not wrestle against flesh and blood, but against principalities, against powers, against the rulers of the darkness of this age, against spiritual hosts of wickedness in the heavenly places." Therefore take up the whole armor of God, that you may be able to withstand in the evil day and having done all, to stand. Stand therefore, having **girded your waist with truth,** having **put on the breast plate of righteousness,** and having **shod your feet with the preparation of the gospel of peace;** above all, **taking the shield of faith** with which you will be able to quench all the fiery darts of the wicked one. And **take the helmet of salvation,** and the **sword of the Spirit,** which is the Word of God; **praying always with all prayer and supplication in the Spirit, being watchful to this end with all perseverance and supplication for all the saints."* (Ephesians 6:10-18 NKJV) Emphasis is mine.

As we go forth in spiritual warfare, we must realize that this subject not only deals with the devil and his demons, but also us! Two elements of spiritual warfare that we *must* contend for:

- Taking control of our minds (see Romans 12:1-2).
- Crucifying the flesh (holiness is the way).

In light of this, we must keep in mind that these two elements of spiritual warfare are just as important as the first. The truth of the matter is the devil's attacks against us would not work:

- If our *flesh* did not cooperate.
- If we were truly mortifying (putting to death) sin in the flesh *daily* (see Colossians 3:5)
- If we are living lives that are "dead to sin." (see Romans 6:2)
- If as the Spirit and the Word working in tandem commands – we will not respond to demonic suggestions and fleshly temptations.

Dead people can't respond to anything. Here then is the power for living a crucified life!

SLAM THE DOORS

A very popular truth (for believers) concerning spiritual warfare says, "we do not fight to gain victory – but we fight from victory." We have victory in Jesus! Praise God! Someone else might offer something else – seemingly on the right side! But for followers of Christ, victory begins with being on God's side in Christ which is our identity.

The apostle Paul plants our hope in the fact that our salvation has moved us to a new kingdom. Now, as citizens of heaven we have not only a new standard for living, but also an enduring reason to hope. He tells the Colossian believers:

For this cause we also pray, "...*That you might be strengthened with all might, according to His glorious power, for all patience and long-suffering with joy; giving thanks to the Father, who has qualified us to be partakers of the inheritance of the saints in the light. He has delivered us from the power of darkness and conveyed us into the kingdom of the Son of His love.*" (Colossians 1:11-13 NKJV)

Paul passed this same idea along to the Philippians. "Only let your conduct be worthy of the Gospel of Christ, so that whether I come and see you or am absent, I may hear of your affairs, that you stand fast in one spirit, with one mind striving together for the faith of the gospel." (Philippians 1:27 NKJV)

CITIZENS OF GOD'S KINGDOM

As citizens of God's kingdom, we have rights and privileges, responsibilities, and duties to fulfill. But above all, we have the assurance that we live under the protecting hand of the King of all Creation. We have the assurance of *His ultimate victory*. Then the seventh angel sounded: and there were loud voices in heaven, saying,

"The kingdoms of this world have become the kingdoms, of our Lord and of His Christ, and He shall reign forever and ever." (Revelation 11:15 NKJV)

Yes, one day all the battles of this world will be over, all fighting will come to a permanent end, all guns will fall silent, and the mighty Lamb of God will present the kingdom in victory to the Father. In I Corinthians 15, the apostle Paul shows us how all of this comes to a glorious end – as he writes about the change that has come through Jesus' resurrection:

"For as in Adam all die, even so in Christ
shall all be made alive.
But every man in his own order:
Christ the first fruits; afterward they
that are Christ's at His coming.
Then cometh the end when He shall
have delivered up the kingdom of God,
even the Father; when He shall have
put down all rule and all
authority and power.
For He must reign,
till He hath put all enemies

under His feet.
The last enemy that shall be
destroyed is death.
For He hath put all things under His feet.
But when He saith, all things are put
under Him, it is manifest that He is excepted,
which did put all things under Him.
And when all things shall be subdued unto Him,
unto Him that put all things under Him,
that God may be all in all." KJV

STUDY GUIDE: WORKSHEET AND REFLECTIONS
CHAPTER 15

1. We are commanded in the Scripture to deal with the unseen, invisible forces that Satan has brought against us: 1) cast out demons and 2) pull down strongholds see Mark 16:17 and 2 Corinthians 10:3-5 respectively. This is part of our Christian duty and responsibility toward the _____, the _____, and the _____.

2. First John 3:8 says, "…. For this purpose the Son of God was _____, that He might destroy the _____ of Satan.

3. In order to carry out the satanic travesty planed by Satan, his demons and his American cronies would require a _____ religion. That would not be Christianity.

4. So secular humanism takes on the name of "civic religion" with the idea of getting rid of _____ and _____ _____ of _____, mainly His influence from ____ _____ of America's life, so that "self" rules.

5. Satan influences _____ so that they appeal to the sinfulness of human beings.

6. Two elements of spiritual warfare that we must contend for are: 1) control ____ our _____ (see Romans 12:2). And 2) crucifying the _____.

7. The truth of the matter is the devil's attacks against us would not work if our _____ did not _____.

Section Four

LOVE AND HOLINESS

MYSTERIES OF THE KINGDOM

Matthew 13 is one of the most crucial chapters in the Bible, one that every believer should seek to understand thoroughly. The rebellion against Christ reached its peak, and He turned from the nation of Israel – to *all* who will come to Him – He is now speaking of a worldwide family. So, the question is, "What about the kingdom, now that Israel has rejected their King?" The answer to that question is found in Matthew 13: where Christ outlines "the mysteries of the kingdom" and explains what the "kingdom of heaven" is like in the absence of the King during this present *age* of grace (the period between His two Advents). As stated earlier, at the end of chapter 11, Jesus gave an invitation to the Gentile:

"Come to Me, all who labor and are heavy laden, and I will give you rest. Take My yoke upon you, and learn from Me, for I am gentle and lowly in heart, and you will find rest for your souls. For My yoke is easy, and My burden is light." (Matthew 11:28-30 ESV)

THE REASON FOR THE PARABLE

The reason for parables was two-fold: *First,* the human condition
of the people's hearts caused Jesus to use parables. The Jews came
back from Babylon captivity delivered from their sin of idolatry.
Though the "house" was swept clean, it was still empty. The people
had religion and outward morality, but their hearts were empty, and
their religion was vain. Again, the "house" here refers to the literal
house in which Jesus had been teaching – but it can also symbolize
the house of Israel (see 10:6).

Second: By leaving the house, He was symbolically saying, that
He had left the nation of Israel and would now turn to the Gentiles.
Christ quotes Isaiah 6:9-10 to explain why He was using parables:
the hearts, ears, and eyes of the people had become dull, hard, and
blind. A parable is a story in which something familiar (natural) is
used to explain something (spiritual). He was hiding the truth from
the rebellious, but He was exciting those who really wanted to know
the truth. He would not cast these pearls of truth before swine (7:6).

Christ fulfilled the prophecy in Psalm 78:2. The truths given in
Matthew 13 had been kept secret from the foundation of the world;
they were a "mystery" hidden from people – but now revealed.
Please be mindful that "the kingdom of heaven" is not referring to
the kingdom of Christ's 1000-year reign but rather to <u>the kingdom
here on earth during His absence.</u> Once again, the "kingdom of
heaven" is a *mixture* of good and evil, true, and false. It is not the
church! The church is *in* the kingdom of heaven, here on the earth,
but *distinct* from it. The kingdom of heaven is equivalent to our
word "Christendom." Christendom is made up of all who profess
allegiance to the King, whether true or pretenders.

THE PERIOD OF TIME

We can see in Matthew 13 the kingdom of heaven *begins* with
the sowing of the seed (the Word of God in the hearts of people)
in Christ's day and continues to the end of the age. These parables
outline God's program and Satan's opposition throughout this

age (Both the wheat and the tares have grown up). Jesus Himself, explains the symbols used in the parable:

1. The man is Christ (v. 7).
2. The seed is believers, children of the kingdom (v. 38).
3. The field is the world (v. 38).
4. The enemy is Satan (v. 39).
5. The tares are the children of the Satan (v. 39).
6. The reapers are angels (v. 39).
7. The harvest is the end of the age (v. 39).

Satan's Opposition
Satan's Point Of Attack

IN THE INDIVIDUAL IN THE WORLD
Parable of the Sower tares, mustard seed, leaven

THE SEED

Snatches away the seed (WORD) Plants counterfeit Christians – (TARES)

THE GROWTH

Starves the plant Has grotesque growth –
It cannot grow MUSTARD SEED[58]

---

[58]   The conditions to be fulfilled by the mustard are that it should be a familiar plant, with a very small seed (Matt. 17:20; Luke 13:19, 17:6, sown in the earth, growing **larger (grotesque) than** garden herbs, Matt. 13:31, having large branches, Mark 4:30-33 ... attracts passing birds, someone has said, buzzards, attaining the height of 10-12 feet tall). As the parable (see Matt. 13:31-32; 17:20) indicates, **Christendom** presents a sort of **Christianity** that has become *conformed to the principles and ways of the world, and the world has favored this **debased Christianity.*** Contrast the testimony of the New Testament, see John 17:14; Galatians 6:14; 1 Peter 2:11; 1 John 3:1. VINE'S Complete Expository Dictionary of OLD and NEW Testament Words (Thomas Nelson Publishers, Nashville, 1984) 423.

THE FRUIT

Smothers the fruit (unfruitful) Injects false doctrine – (leaven)

Wherever Christ "plants" true believers to bear fruit for His glory, Satan plants his false counterfeits who opposes the work and hinders the harvest. Christians are seeds, and the kingdom of heaven is a *mixture* of the true seed (Christians) and the counterfeit (children of the devil). Knowing this that, Satan is a "liar and the father of lies" (John 8:44), we need to constantly monitor ourselves against falsehood and deception, especially when it comes to our self-understanding. We must tell ourselves *the truth* about who we are and resist acting contrary to our identity *in Christ*. Certainly, the Bible gives us a number of affirmations concerning our identity and value in Christ. A brief look at the Scriptures reveals that:

- We are the salt of the earth (Matthew 5:13).
- We are the light of the world (Matthew 5:14).
- We are joint heirs with Christ Jesus (Romans 8:17).
- We are subject to God's special care (1 Peter 5:6-7).
- We are the children of God (1 John 3:1).

We will cut the list at this point, but these alone should encourage us and give us a solid anchor in the storms of life and demonic subjective temptations. Again, the Holy Spirit indwell all followers of Christ – making us temples of the Holy Spirit (see 1 Corinthians 6:19). He is our strength! Thank you, Father.

YOUR SPIRITUAL ARMOR

God has not left us naked before the enemy; He has provided us with spiritual weaponry that has the ability to counterattack and defeat *any* scheme that the devil would try to use against us. God knows that in order for us to be overcomers in any engagement with the unseen powers that have been rallied against us, we must have His supernatural power and special anointing that He has provided for this fight. Paul deals with key elements of spiritual warfare that we need to know and secure in our personal lives. At the outset, we see that God provided the whole armor but we as individual soldiers have to take it up (put it on) In Ephesians 6:14-18, Paul admonishes us to:

*"Therefore, take up the whole armor of God, that you may be able to withstand **in the evil day,** and having done all, to stand. Stand therefore, having girded your **1) waist with truth,** having put on the **2) breastplate of righteousness,** and having shod your feet with the preparation of the **3) gospel of peace;** above all, taking the **4) shield of faith** with which you will be able to quench all the fiery darts of the wicked one. And take the **5) helmet of salvation,** and the **6) sword of the Spirit,** which is the **Word of God. Praying always with all prayer and supplication in the Spirit ....** (NKJV).* Emphasis is mine throughout.

The purpose for which we are given the *whole* armor of God to put on – so that we may be able to stand *against* the wiles of the devil."

Paul describes this weaponry as "the whole armor of God." Because this weaponry has its origin in God, it is key that we remain in unbroken fellowship with God in order for us to continually reap the benefits of our spiritual armor. If we break fellowship with the Lord, we step away from our all-important *Power Source.* However, as long as our fellowship is unbroken, our spiritual weaponry also remains connected.

Today many people ignore their spiritual lives and cease to walk in the power of the Holy Spirit – then complain because the bottom has fallen out opening up all kinds of trouble in their lives. This outbreak of confusion happens when the believer ceases to walk under the guidance in fellowship with and in the power of God. He or she is choosing to temporarily move away from the Source from which their armor comes! Stepping away from fellowship with the Lord, the believer temporarily stops the flow of this divine power into his or her life.

Although the power of God is still available to the believer – if we develop an "I don't care attitude" God pulls the plug. This voluntary disobedience suspends his or her ability to walk in the armor of God – the very armor that God gave to protect and defend us. Why? Because spiritual armor originated in the Lord. Please know, that ongoing fellowship with God is your absolute guarantee that you are habitually and constantly dressed in the *whole* armor of God. After laying down your armor temporarily, you will only be able to pick it up again when you repent and begin to walk in fellowship with the Lord once again.

It is so sad that some denominations, and Para-ministries have chosen to use only a certain part or parts of the armor of God. Some teach on the "shield of faith" and the "sword of the Spirt" while neglecting the other pieces of armor. Remember, God has given us everything we need to successfully fight opposing spiritual forces.

THE BATTLEFIELD OF THE MIND

As I pointed out earlier, spiritual warfare is primarily a matter of the mind. As long as the mind is renewed to *right thinking by the Word of God,* most of the attacks will fail. Warning! Do not leave your mind open and unguarded – it becomes the main battlefield the devil uses to destroy emotions, lives, finances, businesses, marriages, whole families. This is why to "stand guard" over your mind is one of the believer's essential responsibilities (see Romans 12:1, 2).

In doing so, you are actually placing a guard around every other battlefield in your life! Keep in mind the devil does not want you to fulfill your calling (assignment) in the body of Christ – yet you must stand guard until it is completed. Until the job is completed, and the battle is won, you must stand guard over the will of God for your life. This is the responsibility of every believer.

Remember the most important battlefield of your life is your mind!

Prayer – the ultimate weapon

Prayer is at the very center of all aspects of spiritual warfare and life. When we keep our attention focused on the Lord, instead of being overwhelmed by the enemy. It is our only means of continued supply, direction, and restoration in the battle. Prayer is our lifeline to the Throne of Grace. It is not by chance that Paul concludes his exhortation on spiritual armor emphasizing the urgency of prayer. "Pray at all times in the Spirit, with all prayer and supplication. To that end, keep alert with all perseverance, making supplication for all the saints." (Ephesians 6:18 ESV) One writer put it this way:

The effect of prayer is union with God, and, if someone is with God, he is separated from the enemy!

The exhortation to "pray always" is repeated several times in Scripture. (see Luke 18:1; I Thessalonians 5:17) What may seem difficult has actually been commanded by our Lord. We must make prayer our first response – not our last resort. So many times, however, we rely on every other possible solution before turning to prayer. When all human options are exhausted, we finally turn to God. We must train ourselves to pray first honestly and continually. Through prayer we guard our holiness.

It makes us forget injuries, defeats in justice, and repent for sin. Prayer will lift you when you are weary and comfort you when you are downhearted. Prayer is the present enjoyment and the substance of future good things to come.

We overcome Satan

And I heard a loud voice in heaven saying, "Now the salvation and the power and the kingdom of our God and the authority of his Christ have come, for the accuser of our brothers has been thrown down, who accuses them day and night before our God.

1. *And they have conquered [overcame him] by the blood of the Lamb and by*
2. *the word of their testimony*
3. *for they loved not their lives even unto death."* (they Revelation 12:10-11 ESV) Emphasis added.

Satan and his demons have made it their top priority to accuse you twenty-four hours a day. However, the text above from Revelation reminds us how to respond to his attacks while armed in the full armor of God. The devil is overcome by three principles. I want to point out, the text says, *"they conquered (overcame) him"* by these three things:

1. The Blood of the Lamb (Christ)

The Lamb referred to in this passage is Christ, who was slain from the foundation of the world. (see Revelation 13:8) Sadly, many Christians do not understand the blood. We sing, *"There is power in the blood"* or *"the blood will never lose its power"* – but what makes Jesus different from any other man is He is the Lamb of God!

Nothing but the blood of Jesus, shed in His death, for sin, can cover sin on God's side or remove it on our side.

We find the same teaching in the writings of the apostles. Paul wrote of *"being justified freely by his grace through the redemption that is in Christ Jesus ... through faith in his blood."* (see Romans 3:24-25), and of *"being now justified by his blood."* (see Romans 5:9)

To the Corinthians, Paul declared that the *"cup of blessing which we bless, is ... the communion of the blood of Christ."* (see I Corinthians 10:16)

In the epistle to the Galatians, he used the word *cross* to convey the same meaning (see, for example, Galatians 6:14), while in Colossians he united the two words and spoke of *"the blood of the cross."* (see Colossians 1:20)

He reminded the Ephesians that *"we have redemption through his blood"* (see Ephesians 1:7) and that we *"are made nigh by the blood of Christ"* (see Ephesians 2:13).

See how the apostle John assured his *"little children."* (see I John 2:1) that *"the blood of Jesus Christ His Son cleanseth us from all sin."* (see I John 1:7) The Son is He *"that came ... not by water only; but by water and blood."* (see I John 5:6) KJV

Later on, when John saw the great company that no man could number, he was told in reply to his question as to who they were, "[They have] *washed their robes, and made them white in the blood of the Lamb."* (Revelation 7:14 ESV).

All of these writers agreed together in mentioning the blood and in glorying in it as the *power* by which eternal redemption through Christ is fully accomplished and is then applied by the Holy Spirit.

2. The Word of their Testimony

The second way Satan is overcome, according to Revelation 12:11, is in the word "testimony" we find the key component to having one: *"test."* A testimony testifies as to what God has done to bring you through something that no one else could have brought you through. So, if God has never brought you through something – your testimony is going to be kind of vague.

You gain a much more powerful testimony when you know that if God doesn't do something you are going to lose everything – including your mind.

This is when you don't know how you're going to buy your food, pay the rent, get a job, find a spouse, mend your relationship with your spouse. It is these times when God wants us to know that He is the only hope for relief in the crisis. Here is a true testimony when He brings us through it. The Scripture says Satan was overcome by the word of their testimony. They proclaimed what the Lord had done for them that only He could do – He gave them the victory! When Christ gives us a testimony, **we are a testimony,** we are to use it as a counter cultural to overcome the enemy. "**I am a living testimony – are you?**" **Do you give yourself away?**

When we **proclaim Him** and **testify** of what He has done in our lives, that no one else could do – He speaks of us. He said, "*So everyone who acknowledges Me before men, I also will acknowledge before My Father who is in heaven, but whoever denies Me before men, I also will deny before My Father who is in heaven*" (Matthew 10:32-33 ESV). Our denial shows up in His **rejection** of our requests before the Father. Emphasis added throughout.

Without Jesus Christ, I am nothing. Without Jesus Christ, I have no power to overcome Satan and his influence in my life. Jesus did it all by Himself!

When you put on the full armor of God in order to walk in the victory, He has won for you, your advancement in that victory will be tied to the word of your testimony. For some reason, some Christians feel that their testimony is to be given in church only. It's so easy to tell people in church what the Lord has done. But you can overcome Satan in your home, on your job and anywhere else. You can proclaim the testimony of the name of Jesus Christ and your personal identification with Him. Again, in this evil day, we are Christ's counter-cultural!

3. Loving Jesus Christ

The third way Satan is overcome is located at the end of Revelation 12:11, where we are told, "*… for they loved not their lives even unto death.*" (ESV) Their love was so strong, even unto death! This love commitment is so essential that Jesus rebuked the church at Ephesus for leaving their first love (see Revelation 2:4).

Without a loving relationship with Jesus Christ through the atoning work on the cross, you will be overpowered by Satan's demons no matter how loud you shout and call on Jesus.

The authority comes in the relationship. With a proper relationship, we cross over into the heavenly places, where God does exceedingly, abundantly above all that you can ask or think, for His glory. The blood of Jesus Christ gives believers *access* and *authority* in the spiritual realm. When you proclaim these three elements before Satan:

- The blood of Jesus
- Your testimony of Christ
- Your relationship with Christ

Satan is a defeated foe, the only thing he can do is deceive you into thinking you are on your own. With the armor of God in place you will be able to handle in the physical realm whatever Satan throws at you in the spiritual realm. Remember, we were told to "put on" the whole armor of God that we may be able to stand. So, if Satan is running your life, your passions, and emotions – he is influencing decisions. Without a doubt, you have left off a piece of your armor.

God does not dress us in the armor, but He has given us everything we need to put it on in faith. Many times, people have talked about a gift they have received and on occasion just put it on a shelf in the garage, to be checked out later, but one day he needed it, a hurricane had knocked out the area's electricity. He and his son went to the shelf and pulled down the crate that containing a gasoline operated generator, as he uncrated the generator to his amazement two essential parts were missing! We are accountable for all of the armor; the Lord gives us.

The family lost food in the freezer and the refrigerator! *Knowing is key to victory!* We are to put on the full armor of God. Earlier we spoke of walking in the armor of God, we are living in an evil time, so we had better gear up. Without Christ the armor is useless to you. But with Christ we are victorious. When you live in the truth of His atoning blood, proclaiming the word of your testimony, and abide in a true relationship with Him – even demons will flee from you.

The authority is in the relationship – with Christ Jesus!

The armor of God has been completely supplied. Your victory has been completely provided. If you've taken off your armor for any reason, get it back on. But until you get a hold of each piece in faith – they do you no good. Listen! The good news is, only God can provide the armor for you. Praise God, your life will change in a way that only God can get the glory.

Strongholds and problems that you have struggled with for years can be changed overnight when things are carried out God's way. A case in point, a lady bent over for 18 years. Doctors no doubt tried to heal her. However, when Jesus came on the scene, what couldn't be fixed in 18 years was fixed immediately.

On a Sabbath Jesus was teaching in one of the synagogues, and a woman was there who had been crippled by a spirit for eighteen years. She was bent over and could not straighten up at all. When Jesus saw her, He called her forward and said to her, "Woman, you are set free from your infirmity." Then he put His hands on her, and immediately she straightened up and praised God. (Luke 13:10-13 NIV)

You know God intervened when something you have been struggling with for years immediately changes. Friend, you can live in victory that Christ has secured for you because – you trusted in Him!

He crossed you over into a whole new realm. You can defeat your enemy as well. You have a new purpose and a destiny. To glorify God in all that you do while significantly impacting others and the culture around you (God's counter-cultural).

STUDY GUIDE: WORKSHEET AND REFLECTIONS
CHAPTER 16

Matthew 13 is one of the most crucial chapters in the Bible, one that every believer should seek to understand thoroughly. The rebellion against Christ had peaked, and He turned from the nation of Israel – unto all who will come to Him.

1. Matthew 13 explains what the "_____ ____ _____
    " is like in the absence of the King during this present "age of grace"(the period between the two advents).

2. The reason Jesus used the parables was twofold: 1) the condition of the people's _____ 2) He would now turn to the _____.

3. The parables in chapter 13 outline God's _____ and Satan's _____ throughout this age.

4. The kingdom of heaven is a mixture of the _____ _____ and the _____ _____.

5. God provides the whole armor, but we as individual _____ have the responsibility to _____ ____ _____. Prayer is key.

6. It is key that we remain in unbroken _____ with God in order to continually _____ the benefits of our spiritual armor.

7. As stated, spiritual warfare is _____ a matter of the mind. As long as the min is renewed to right thinking by the _____ of _____ most attacks will fail. This is the believer's responsibility (see Romans 12:1-20).

Chapter Seventeen

THE FRUIT OF THE SPIRIT IS LOVE

"For God so loved the world that He gave His only begotten Son, that whoever believes in Him should not perish but have everlasting life." (John 3:16)

When most Christians speak of the fruit of love, they think of developing and cultivating love relationships toward their brothers and sisters in Christ. While this is the command of God to His children, it is not all that is included in love. Each child of God is commanded to diligently care for and develop an individual love relationship with his or her heavenly Father in heaven.

Something else to ponder today is, many Christians do not seem to know that the great Commandment is not, "Love one another." In Matthew 22:37-39, a believer can love the brethren in proper order only after first loving God. Still, some Christians express more love for others in the Body of Christ than they express to God:

Jesus said unto him, Thou shalt love the Lord thy God with all thy heart, and with all thy soul, and with all thy mind. This is the first commandment. And the second is like unto it, Thou shalt love thy neighbor as thyself. (KJV)

Most Christians feel quite comfortable in sitting down, conversing, and expressing their love to other members of the Body of Christ. How would they act if Jesus Christ (in the flesh) walked into the church. And sat down to converse with them. How comfortable would they be? Well, my family and I experienced that very scene in a U.S. Army Garrison Chapel worship service in Seoul, Republic of Korea in the early 1980s. As we worshipped, the lights dimmed, and a dim spotlight fell on a figure moving slowly forward as the light gradually grew brighter a man entering the sanctuary dressed and made-up just like the picture sold everywhere in that day as the picture of Jesus Christ.

Making this presentation was a professional actor from Hollywood California. I don't know if anyone knew this was going to happen, but the highest-ranking officer present was our Commanding General, a four-star General. The entire congregation fell silent as this man emerged into the light. This entire event was over in a few seconds. I do not remember whether the Chaplain got around to preaching that morning, but it certainly impacted the people. I was on usher duty with some of the other men, I do not remember any conversing as we gathered our families and departed the Sanctuary. That was a great revival? A lot of soul searching went on that day.

There really is no single explanation for some of God's beloved believers finding it easier to express more love to one another than to their Father Who loves them so much that He gave His only begotten Son to die for them (see John 3:16). Sadly, this is still the case with many in the faith community today. In reality most believers would be uncomfortable in a one-on-one encounter with Jesus?

Do you know Him?

God desires that His children know Him to the extent that they are as comfortable loving Him as they are in their closest, most intimate relationship on earth. Only then will believers, the children of God come to know the Father in the Spirit as well as they know the people precious to them in the flesh. At that time, the children of

God get to know the Father in the Spirit as they know their dearest friends and loved ones in the flesh.

Knowing the Father intimately on the earth is your source of assurance and confidence when we each stand before the Son of God on the day that is imminent. (see John 14:8, 9)

Today many people rely totally on expressing their love to the Father indirectly through doing good works. In that day when they stand before Him, will be rejected.

In Matthew 7:22, Jesus said, "Many will say to me in that day, Lord, Lord, have we not prophesied in thy name? And in thy name have cast out devils? And in thy name done many wonderful works? According to Jesus, one basis of His rejection of such people will be expressed in the words, ... **I never knew[59] you** ... (v. 23)

Jesus will be saying: *"I never got to know you, for you did not cultivate that **fruit of love** and **develop an intimate, loving relationship with Me."** Therefore, it will greatly benefit us believers in that day if we will begin to develop a love relationship with the Father by cultivating this all-important *fruit of love* today. Again, Christ is our example in love relationship:

- He loved the Father (see John 14:31; 6:38).
- He loved the Scriptures (Matthew 5:17-18; Luke 4:16-21; 24:44-45; John 10:34-36).
- He loved His own disciples (John 13:1; 15:9; Romans 8:37-39).
- He loves the Church as His own Bride (Ephesians 5:25-27).
- He loves all men regardless of the color of their skin (Mark 10:21; Matthew 11:19; John 10:11; 15:13; Romans 5:8).
- He loved His enemies (Matthew 5:43-48; Luke 22:51; 23:34; Matthew 26:50).
- He prayed that this love would be in us (John 17:26; 13:34-35).

---

[59] This Greek word for **knew** is *ginosko* which means "to know by experience or effort; knowledge as the result of prolonged practice; knowledge grounded in personal experience; to get to know.

- He was continually moved with compassion towards others (John 11:35; 6:5; Mark 6:34; Matthew 8:16; 20:34; Luke 4:41; 5:12-15)

The people are dying of *spiritual starvation* because they do not know the Bible's full story, and thus they do not find themselves in the story. Certainly, they know a lot of little stories. They have some knowledge, but that is not the big picture. So, as we preach and teach, we must bring every text into accountability with the full story of Scripture. We must help our people to know the beginning, the middle, and the end – creation, fall, redemption, and consummation. This way, you will show your people who they are and where they are going.

THE DECONSTRUCTION OF TRUTH

Throughout past centuries the nature of truth has been debated, focused on competitive claims to truth. However, today postmodernists reject the very notion truth as absolute, fixed, universal, or objective. The Christian (tradition) understands truth as *established by God* and known to us through revelation of the Holy Spirit in Scripture.

Truth is eternal, fixed, and universal, and we are responsible to order our minds in line with God's revealed truth and then to bear witness to this truth. Modern science, itself a product of the Enlightenment, *rejected biblical revelation as a source of truth* and put the scientific method in its place. Modernists were confident that their approach would yield *objective and universal truths by means of human reason.*

Post modernists *reject* both the Christian and modernist approaches to truth. According to postmodern theory, truth is not universal, is not objective or absolute, and cannot be determined by a commonly accepted method. Instead, postmodernists argue that truth is *relative, plural, and inaccessible to universal reason.* As philosopher Richard Rorty suggests:

- Truth is made rather than found.

- All truth is socially constructed.
- Social groups construct their own "truth" to serve their own interests.
- What is "true" for one group is not necessarily "true" for any other.
- Therefore, all claims to truth are constructed to serve those in power. Therefore, the role of the intellectual is to destruct truth claims in order to liberate the society.
- Truth is not universal, for every culture establishes own truth. Nor is truth objectively real, for all truth is merely constructed. In other words, it is *made,* not *found.*[60]

Little imagination is needed to see that this radical relativism is a *direct* challenge to the Christian gospel.

The Christian understands truth as established by God and known to us through the self-revelation of God in Scripture. Truth is eternal, fixed, and universal, and our responsibility is to order our minds in accordance with God's revealed truth and then to bear witness to that truth in conduct and life.

---

[60] R. Albert Mohler Jr. *He is not Silent, "Preaching in a Postmodern World"* (Moody Publishers, Chicago, IL. 2008) 116-117.

STUDY GUIDE: WORKSHEET & REFLECTIONS CHAPTER 17

1. Christians express more _____ for others in the Body of Christ than they _____ to God.

2. Knowing the Father intimately on earth is your source of _____ and _____ when we each stand before the Son of God on the day that is imminent.

3. Today many people rely totally on expressing their _____ to the Father indirectly through doing good works. In that day they will be _____.

4. We must help our people to know the beginning, the middle, and the end (the full story) – creation, fall, redemption, and _____.

5. Truth is _____, fixed, and universal, and we are responsible to order our minds in _____ with God's revealed truth.

6. Modern science, itself a product of the Enlightenment, rejected biblical revelation as a _____ of _____ and put the scientific method in its place.

7. Modernists were confident their approach would yield
_____ and _____ _____ by means
of human reason.

8. Post modernists reject both the Christian and modernist
approaches to _____.

OUT OF BABYLON

And he cried mightily with a loud voice saying, "Babylon the great is fallen, is fallen, and has become a dwelling place of demons, a prison for every foul spirit, and a cage for every unclean and hated bird! For all the nations have drunk of the wine of the wrath of her fornication, the kings of the earth have committed fornication with her, and the merchants of the earth have become rich through the abundance of her luxury." (Revelation 18:2-3 NKJV)

In Revelation, the world in rebellion against God is called "Babylon." The Old Testament prophets frequently prophesied the fall of Babylon, the capital, of the empire that destroyed the City of God, Jerusalem, and carried His people away as captives. (see Isaiah 14:21; 21:9; Jerimiah 50:9; 52:37) Additionally, Babylon is a word picture for a society that persecuted God's people, but that God will eventually destroy.

BABYLON IN THE BEGINNING

Originally, Babylon was more than a wealthy, glamorous city – it was primarily a religious city. To understand this gives us great insight into the *nature* of this enemy. Genesis 11:4 tells us the common intent of the Babylonian people was to build themselves a city, *"and a tower whose top will reach into heaven."* With their advance skills in art and warfare – their *pride* was in their religion. When God confused their language and scattered them across the earth, the <u>spirit of Babylon</u> spread throughout the world; along with the desire to *"reach into heaven"* through fabricated initiatives in every nation. We also see in this spirit the ambition to *"make a name for themselves."* King Solomon observed, *"that all toil and all skill in work come from a man's envy of his neighbor."* (Eccl. 4:4 ESV)

THE SPIRIT OF BABYLON

Rivalry and the desire to "make a name for oneself" still make up the nature of the spirit of Babylon. Another comment about the beginnings of Babylon: the Scripture says the people journeyed east to the land of Shinar and **"settled there"** (see Genesis 11:2). Once a church stop pressing on the upward way and begins to "settle down," watch out! Something Babylonish in spirit and nature is about to rise up. We can recognize the influence of Babylon in any group or church that offer "lip service" to God, a far-off deity whose dwelling place is not with men. In contrast, Jesus is our Emmanuel, *"God with us!"*

The very essence of true Christianity is Christ in us – the hope of glory! Notice, you can discern the spirit of Babylon in a church that honors God in heaven without having any relationship with Him on earth. That I feel is most depressing of all the other crisis and they are many.

TODAY'S CHALLENGES TO THE CHURCH

Today, more than ever, we are entering times of great and increasing intensifying challenges for the Christian church. Even the man in the street is beginning to believe that the end may be sooner than we think! The pandemic is not the measure for the ever-widening crisis we are experiencing in the present hour as we witness the collateral damage resulting from the rapid decline of Christianity and collapse of Christian influence in the world (Babylon). Churches are emptying all across America and other nations in the Western world as man like the devil tries to put himself and his agenda above God, the Creator and owner of all. The spirit of Babylon is spreading secularism, digital postmodernism, unbelief and mixed beliefs[61] around the world like wildfire.

As I stated in an earlier section, a generation has turned its back on God, Christ, the Holy Spirit, and the body of Christ (the church). The result is an epidemic of opioids, and other addictions, suicides, homicides, and violent people. All across our society even in our churches we are seeing fewer marriages, empty cradles, as cohabitation has become more acceptable than traditional marriages. As love grows colder with each passing day, we see deeper and more violence systemic racial strife and division among the nations.

Like the fading church wedding, funerals in churches are on the low side as elaborate funeral homes with sizable chapels appear everywhere, cremations, and graveside ceremonies eliminate the need for a Christian pastor or church funeral as well. It is common to work with and be around people today who admit they have never been inside of a traditional church building, because they never had a reason to go there. Eventually, that is if the Lord tarries, the faith community will hopefully realize that the Great Commission Jesus gave to His disciples (including us) was "Go!" and make disciples, not "come and sit." It's time to come out of our forts and bunkers take the ministry on the (counter-offense) back to the streets where the objective (mission) is!

"Hear what the Spirit is saying to the churches!"

I see the church in three phases, all three are concerned with winning souls to Christ. The apostle Peter "Go into all the world (Babylon) and preach the gospel. Then the apostle Paul came along planting the church, establishing, and teaching, (experiencing the encounter) in all that Christ commanded, then the apostle John (the

---

[61]   A smorgasbord a mixture of different beliefs, religions, and thoughts.

net mender) came along to repair the net, to save, heal (restore), and mature for (deployment) ministry of church, and counter the world of darkness. I recently read a reputable poll news report that stated, usually each year in this country, a number of churches close their doors for assorted reasons; but were countered by an equal amount of new church plants to replace them, however, that has changed significantly today to say – there are more churches closings than there are new churches opening.

THE GOSPEL INVITATION

I believe, it is now time to grow smaller and deeper, rather than larger and shallower. If Jesus is on the outside knocking – what is going on inside without Him? The picture hanging in many living rooms across the world depicts Christ as standing at the door of the lukewarm church knocking – another interpretation has Him knocking at the door of human hearts. (see Revelation 3:20)

"Behold, I stand at the door and knock. If anyone hears My voice and opens the door, I will come in to him and dine with him, and he with Me." (Revelation 3:20 NKJV)

Verse 20 is often used as a gospel invitation. It is important to note that in this verse Christ's purpose for entry is renewed fellowship. This church was addressed differently than the other six – the name "Laodicea" means "the *rule* of the people" and suggests a church that no longer follows spiritual leaders or the authority of the Word of God. The church's condition is "lukewarm" that comes from mixing hot and cold. It is a church that has been polluted with error (the spirit of Babylon). We find this church in every city and town, USA. Sadly, like the church of the Laodiceans, it is "rich" but in reality do not know that really they are poor, pitiful, blind, and naked. This church depicts the apostate church of today, with its prestige, wealth, and political power – yet all the while spiritually poor and blind. Remember, the spirit of Babylon? Remember the *world in rebellion* against God, is called (Babylon)!

The city of Laodicea was known for its wool, wealth, and medicine, so Christ used those images in v. 18. Christ wanted to give them,

- The true riches of the Word of God
- The garments of grace and
- The ability to see spiritual things

This church has wealth and power, but no Christ. He is willing to come into the life of one person – if that person will but invite Him. How tragic that a church can become so *lukewarm* and so *proud* that Christ has to leave the assembly and stand outside. There was something wrong with their values, vestures, and their vision. If they would not *repent,* He would chastise them in love. They are indifferent toward Christ and the things of Christ. He is left outside of their plans and programs – and their hearts. As these churches existed in the apostle John's day, so they exist today.

We have busy churches that have left their first love (Ephesus) – but accept they *repent* and *return to their first love* – more than likely they will become lukewarm toward Christ. False doctrine begins small, but unless countered it will infect the entire assembly. Praise God there is a remnant of true believers (the overcomers) in each church who are responsible to be faithful to Christ until He returns.

THE IMPORTANCE OF THE WORD OF GOD

The importance of the Word of God to the churches is critical today. Seven times Christ calls the churches to *"hear what the Spirit is saying."* When churches stop listening to the voice of the Spirit through the Word and begin to listen to the voices of false teachers – they begin to turn from the truth. We must keep the faith (2:32), even at the cost of our lives. We must keep His Word (3:8, 10), and never, never deny His name! Apart from the Word of God and the Spirit working in tandem in and through us – there is no life or hope for the churches. Amen.

STUDY GUIDE: WORKSHEET & REFLECTIONS CHAPTER 18

1. In Revelation, the world in rebellion against God is called _____.

2. The common intent of the Babylonian people was to build themselves a city and a _____ to _____.

3. When God confused their language and scattered them across the earth the _____ of _____ spread throughout the world.

4. The word "Laodicea" means _____ of the _____.

5. Explain the Laodicean church's condition:

6. The _____ of _____ is critical today.

7. There is a _____ of believers in _____ _____.

Chapter Nineteen

HOLY UNTO THE LORD

But just as He who called you is holy, so be
holy in all you do; for it is written:
"Be holy, because I am holy."
– 1 Peter 1:15-16

As stated in an earlier chapter, we are family, but we are a special kind of family. We are to be a holy family! Upon God's establishing Israel as His chosen people, He let them know that their *witness* meant to be a *display of God's holiness* to one another – and to the world. He told them to be holy because He is holy. "And the LORD spoke to Moses, saying, *"Speak to all the congregations of the people of Israel and say to them, you shall be holy, for I the Lord your God am holy."* (Leviticus 19:1-2 ESV)

BECAUSE HE IS HOLY

What makes us unique is being saved and in right relationship the Lord Jesus Christ, our Savior the author and finisher of our faith. Isn't it amazing that the command begins with holiness as a description of the character He requires for His people. The word holiness means *"to cut."* To set apart or cut something off from something that it was originally a part of or connected to make it unique. Although there may be some similarities to what it was cut away from, it is no longer connected to what it was cut from.

When God came and pulled us out of the world from whence, we came, He cut us away from what we were. He uniquely cut us away to:

- Wear the kingdom uniform
- Be obedient to the Word of God
- Bring about healing
- Be a peacemaker
- Bring about change
- Be family
- Be something new

"Therefore, if anyone is in Christ, *he or she* is a new creature; the old things passed away; behold, new things have come." (2 Corinthians 5:17 NASB) A holy God having uniquely cut us away to be distinct. Therefore, arrogance, pride, greed, or licentiousness have passed away and no longer identifies us. How can we dare be otherwise?

In his book, *One Blood: Parting Words to the Church on Race,* Dr. Perkins said of himself and his friend of more than twenty years: "When I think of what made our love grow more and more, it was whenever we were together, we were competing to love the other more."[62] Actually, God has already given us what we need. Throughout this book it's repeated, "We fight from victory, not to victory."

LIVING HOLY

The world should see the children of God as a city on a hill. We are to demonstrate by how we love God, the people of God, and the non-believer. The command was to love God's people and the non-believer. *"Now when you reap the harvest of your land, you shall not*

---

[62] John M. Perkins, *One Blood: Parting Words to the Church on Race* (Chicago: Moody Publishers, 2018) 166-167.

reap to the very edges of your field, nor shall you gather the gleanings your harvest. And you shall not glean your vineyard, nor shall you gather the fallen grapes of you vincyard; You shall leave them for the needy and for the stranger. I am the LORD your God." (Lev. 19:9-10 NASB)

HOLINESS IS NOT OPTIONAL

The holiness of God is an exceedingly high standard, a perfect standard. But nonetheless one that He holds us to. He can do no less. While it is true that He accepts us solely through the merit of Christ, God's standard for our character, our attitudes, affections, and actions is, "Be holy because I am holy." We must take this seriously if we are to grow in holiness. The writer of Hebrews admonishes us all to,

"Pursue peace with all people, and holiness, without which no one will see the Lord: looking carefully lest anyone fall short of the grace of God; lest any root of bitterness springing up cause trouble, and this many become defiled." (Hebrews 12:14-15 NKJV) Emphasis added.

All believers should be motivated to lay aside every weight, and sin which so easily ensnares us, and *run* with endurance the race that is set before us, looking unto Jesus, the author and finisher of our faith (see 12:1-2). The cloud of witnesses spoken of in this passage refers to those people of faith in Hebrews 11. Certainly, they are not actually spectators watching us, they are witnesses testifying to the truth of the faith in v.2. Earlier, we read the words, *"without holiness no one can see the Lord."* What does this actually mean? First, it does not mean that in the final analysis our salvation depends on some degree or attaining some level of personal holiness.

The best Christians can never merit their salvation through their personal holiness. The Scripture says, "Our righteous deeds are like filthy rags in the light of God's holy law" (see Isaiah 64:6) Our best works are stained with sin. An old saint many centuries ago is credited with this saying, "Even our tears of repentance need to be washed in the blood of the Lamb."

Second, Scripture repeatedly speaks of the obedience and righteousness of Jesus Christ on our behalf,

"For as by one man's disobedience many were made sinners, so also by one Man's obedience many will be made righteous." (Romans 12:19 NKJV)
"For Christ also suffered <u>once</u> for sins, the just for the unjust, that He might bring us to God, being put to death in the flesh but made alive in the Spirit." (I Peter 3:18 NKJV)

These two passages of Scripture teaches us a twofold aspect of Christ's work on our behalf. They are often referred to as His active obedience, and His passive obedience. Christ's death on the Cross was a once-for-all event.

- His active obedience – refers to Christ's sinless life, here on the earth. His perfect obedience and absolute holiness. This credited life He passes on to all who trusts in Him for salvation.
- His passive obedience – refers to His death on the Cross through which He paid in full the penalty for our sins and the wrath of God toward us. We are told in Hebrews 10:5-9, that Christ came to do the *will* of the Father.

The writer goes on to say, "And by that *will*, we have <u>been made holy through the sacrifice of the body of Jesus Christ once for all.</u>" (see Hebrews 10:10) Therefore, we see that our holiness before God depends entirely on the work of Jesus Christ for us – by God's will. That leads to the question, Does Hebrews 12:14 refer then to this holiness which we have in Christ? No, for now the writer speaks of a holiness we are to strive after; we are to *"make every effort … to be holy."* And without holiness, the writer says, no one will see the Lord. Hold onto your hats, the Scripture speaks of both a holiness which we have in Christ before God – and a holiness which we are to strive after daily. These to aspects of holiness fully complement one another, for our salvation is a salvation to holiness:

- "For God did not call is to be impure – but to live a holy life." (see I Thessalonians 4:7)
- Paul wrote to the Corinthians: "To the church of God in Corinth, to those <u>sanctified</u> (made) in Christ Jesus and <u>called</u> (practice) *to be holy in our daily lives.*" (see I Corinthians 1:2)[63]

Christ died that we can be reconciled to
God. Give Him Praise and Glory!

DEAD TO SIN BUT ALIVE TO CHRIST

We saw our **1st** point in Romans 6:11 in an earlier section, how God has delivered us from the realm and reign of sin through union with Christ in His death. We were slaves to sin and in slavery we committed sins. We developed sinful habits regardless of how "good" we *thought* we were. But Jesus Christ came into this sinful world and took our place on the Cross.

He died to sin and through our union with Him we died to sin also.

We were slaves to sin and in slavery we committed sins. Now we are delivered from sin's reign. We are to count on this fact and *resist* sin – so that it does not reign in our mortal bodies. We saw how sin still clings to our bodies waging spiritual warfare through evil desires and deception in our minds. Remember, in regeneration, we are born again in our spirit, therefore our soul and body are not fully committed, and has to be quickened by the Spirit and the Word working in tandem.

---

[63] The word sanctified here means "made holy." That is to say, we are *made holy* through Christ in our standing before God and *called* to be holy in our daily lives. The indwelling Holy Spirit in our lives make us holy in practice.

To experience practical, everyday holiness, we must accept the fact that God has seen fit to allow our daily battle with sin. But praise be to God, that He doesn't leave us to do battle alone. Just as He has delivered us from the overall reign of sin – so He has made provision for us to win the daily firefights. God delivers us from sin's reign, and into the reign of His Son.

Here we arrive at point **#2** in Romans 6:11. We are **not just dead to sin** (see Romans 5), but **we are alive to God** (see Romans 6). We have been brought into the kingdom of Christ. What is so important about being alive unto God in our striving for holiness? For one thing, it means *we are united with Christ in all His power,* Certainly, we know that we *cannot live a holy life in our own strength.* It is not as Satan and the world would have you to think, Christianity is not a do-it-*yourself*-operation.

Now notice, the attitude of Paul to the Philippians 4:11-13. He speaks here about how he has *learned* to be content whatever the circumstances God allows for me. Paul said he could respond with confidence because Christ gave the necessary strength. On another occasion, Paul said he prayed that the Colossians would be, *"being strengthened with all power, according to his glorious might, for all endurance and patience with joy."* (Colossians 1:11 ESV)

Consider again another prayer Paul prayed in his letter to the Ephesians. He said he was praying for them *"that according to the riches of his glory he may grant you to be strengthened with power through his Spirit in your inner being."* (Ephesians 3:16 ESV) He ended the prayer by acknowledging that God *"is able to do far more abundantly than all that we ask or think, according to the power at work within us."* (Ephesians 3:20) Emphasis mine throughout.

GOD EXPECTS EVERY CHRISTIAN TO LIVE A HOLY LIFE!

THE STRUGGLE WITH SIN

Although our union with Christ in His death delivered us from dominion of sin. We still find sin struggling to gain control over us. As Paul pointed out:

"God has not called us for impurity but in holiness. Therefore, whoever disregards this, disregards not man but God, who gives His Holy Spirit to you." (1 Thessalonians 4:7-8 ESV)

Here, Paul introduces the giving of the Holy Spirit for help in our living a holy life by making us holy as He conforms us to the character of Christ. For example, we are told to *flee* sexual immorality because:

- Our bodies are *temples of the Holy Spirit*. (see 1 Corinthians 6:18-19)
- Additionally, we are controlled not by our sinful nature but by the Spirit – if the Spirit of God resides in us. (see Romans 8:9)
- We are told to, "Walk by the Spirit, and you will not gratify the desires of (sinful) flesh. For the desires of the flesh are against the Holy Spirit, and the desires of the Spirit are against the flesh, for these are opposed to each other, to keep you from doing the things you want to do. But if you are led by the Spirit, you are not under the law."(Galatians 2:16-18 ESV)

Growing in the Christian Life

Because we are "alive to God," the Holy Spirit lives within us to *strengthen* us toward holiness. Remember, this teaching is not optional, or something to be put away to a "someday category," the *fact* that we are dead to sin and alive to God has to be activated in our lives for movement by the Spirit toward holiness:

- He enables us to see our *need* for holiness.
- He gives us understanding to see God's standards of holiness.
- He points out our particular areas of sin.

None of this can be understood or exposed except by the Holy Spirit. I repeat, the Bible says, "The heart is deceitful above all things and beyond cure. Who can understand it?" (see Jeremiah 17:9) Naturally, as we see God's standard versus our sinfulness – the desire to be holy awaken in us. Forget not, that we must "will" before we begin to "act" on this! As I stated earlier, I don't remember a day of my life growing up that my father was not a pastor; and his holy life was my constant counsel. Praise God!

I remember the old saints standing in prayer meeting week after week voicing their determination and resolve to spend eternity in heaven with their Lord and Savior, Jesus Christ. Going with dad on occasion to visit the sick and shut-in, on several occasions I witnessed joy and sadness in the room as the saints departed this life. Our father drilled into us, "that death is a part of living!" Someone said, "Live right and you will die right!"

As we grow in the Christian life today, let us pray that the Holy Spirit will strengthen us with holy "boldness." The unholy trinity consisting of the world, the flesh, and the devil seem to be making their last stand – knowing their time is short!

STUDY GUIDE: WORKSHEET & REFLECTIONS CHAPTER 19

1. Upon establishing Israel as His chosen people, God let them know their _____ was meant to be a display of holiness to _____ _____ and the world.

2. Holiness is a description of the _____ He requires of His people.

3. While it is true that God accepts us solely through the merit of Christ, God's standard for our character, our attitudes, affections, and actions is "_____ because ____ ____ _____."

4. The holiness of God is an exceedingly high standard, but nonetheless He _____ _____ ____.

5. Christ died to sin and through our union with Him we died to sin also!

6. Because we are "alive to God," the Holy Spirit lives within us to strengthen _____ _____ _____.

7. The fact that we are dead to sin and alive to God has to be activated in our lives for movement by the _____ toward holiness.

Chapter Twenty

LORD HELP MY UNBELIEF!

Jesus said to him, "If you can believe, all things are possible to him who believes." (Mark 9:23 NKJV)

W e are living in the days when many *think* that biblical Christianity," is antiquated, and not good enough for today's situations, so they retreat to science and reason (governed by the five senses). The father in this narrative realized his shortcoming instantly when hearing Jesus' saying: "If you can believe, all things are possible to him [or her] who believes." The father's cry, **"help my unbelief"** expresses a dilemma that even those who believe can be harassed by – doubt and hopelessness. However, notice this man took proper action by appealing to Jesus for help! "Jesus took the boy by the hand and lifted him up, and he arose (see vv. 14-27). There is much meat in these verses for the mature disciples to pass on today!

WHY COULD WE NOT CAST IT OUT?

That question is still echoing throughout *Ecclesia*, the church, today. Later, there is no doubt the now "shook-up" disciples, asked Jesus. Why they were unsuccessful in casting out the demon?

Mainly, because people to this day, don't accept Jesus' response. Jesus said to them, *"This kind can come forth by nothing, but by prayer and fasting."* (v. 29 NKJV)

Prayer and fasting help us to focus our power and full attention on the various resources available in our Great Healer, Jesus Christ! Truths such as these even from Christ's own lips are widely doubted today, as seen in some translations of the Bible today, [fasting has been omitted]. The same is true with us and our struggle against the kingdom of darkness. Satan did not gain any power at the fall and didn't lose any at the cross. The King James Version uses the *Greek* words *dunamis* (power) and *exousia* (authority). In Colossians 1:13, for example, it translates *exousia* as *power which means* **authority**: "Who hath delivered us from the power **(authority)** of darkness, and hath translated us into the kingdom of His dear Son." Likewise, in Matthew 28:18, Jesus was stating that He had taken *back* the *authority* for us that Adam had lost.

If Jesus had stripped Satan of his power (dunamis) as some teach, then Satan would no longer be able to control us; therefore, we could ignore him completely, just as many Christians do. However, Jesus dealt with Satan's authority (exousia), and delivered us from Satan's authority and given us a higher authority in Christ's name – then we (Christians) must exercise that authority over the devil's works and power. When we do, God's awesome power (the Holy Spirit) will back up our authority. Notice, Luke 10:19, using our *authority* over Satan's power:

"Behold, I give you the authority (exousia) to trample on serpents and scorpions, and over all the power (dunamis) of the enemy, and nothing shall by any means hurt you." (NKJV)

Jesus said we have authority ("keys") to "bind" the forces of hell (see Matthew 16:19). The term is *deo,* and means to fasten or tie, as with a chain or cord. The word is also used in legal circles to mean "legally or contractually binding," which no doubt conveys the idea of authority. We can pray with authority, binding or tying Satan legally, and God will back us with His power. So again, what will determines victory for us? The answer is the knowledge of the truth and exercising authority!

TAKING THE OFFENSE

In an earlier section, we dwelt with the six pieces of armor used for the *defense* (see Ephesians 6:14-17). Now we will focus on the weapons for the *offense*. Of the six pieces of armor for the defense, one, the sword of the Spirit which is the [Word of God] is also an offensive weapon! Paul described what God has done for us, as believers, through the death of Christ on the cross – on our behalf, in Colossians 2:13-15:

When you were dead in your sins and in the uncircumcision of your sinful nature, God made you alive with Christ. He forgave us all our sins, having concealed the written code, with its regulations, that was against us and that stood opposed to us; He took it away, nailing it to the cross. And having disarmed the powers and authorities, He made a public spectacle of them, triumphing over them by the cross. (NIV)

Satan is determined to keep all Christians from understanding this fact – because it is the key to his defeat. The great essential fact is this: Christ has already defeated Satan and all his evil powers and authorities totally and forever. He did all of that through His death on the cross, through His shed blood, and through His triumphant resurrection.

To understand how this was accomplished, we must recognize Satan's primary weapon against us is, the weapon of *guilt*. Revelation 12:10 states the following concerning the matter:

Then I heard a loud voice in heaven say, "Now have come the salvation and the power and the kingdom of our God, and the authority of His Christ. For the accuser of our brothers, who accuses them before our God day and night, has been hurled down." (NIV)

We know that Satan is the accuser of the brethren. He has access to the presence of God, and his principle occupation is to accuse us who believe in Jesus Christ. His sole purpose is *to make us feel guilty.* So long as Satan can keep us feeling guilty – we cannot defeat him. Guilt then is the key to our defeat!

So long as Satan can keep us feeling guilty – we cannot defeat him. Guilt is the key to our defeat, and righteousness is the key to our victory!

Through the death of Jesus Christ in our stead, as our representative, carrying our guilt and paying our penalty – God is now able to forgive us for all our sinful acts. Because His justice has been satisfied by the death of Christ, He can forgive every sin we have committed without compromising His own justice. We must understand that all past sinful acts no matter how many or how serious, have been forgiven. Colossians 2:13 says, *"He forgave us all our sins"* (NIV) when we put our faith in Jesus Christ. Then God made provision for the future (see v. 14):

> *Having canceled the written code, with its regulations,*
> *that was against us and that stood opposed to us*
> *He took it away, nailing it to the cross.* (NIV)

The *"written code"* is the Law of Moses. Jesus, on the cross, did away with the Law of Moses as a requirement for obtaining righteousness with God. As long as the Law of Moses was a requirement, every time one broke even one of the most minor requirements, they were guilty before God. But when the Law was taken out of the way as a requirement for achieving righteousness. Then, provision was made for us to live free from guilt because our faith is reckoned to us for righteousness. There are two other passages, the first is:

> *For Christ is the end of the law for righteousness to everyone who believes.* (Romans 10:4 NASB)

The second Scripture is:

God made Him who had no sin to be sin for us, so that in him we might become the righteousness of God. (2 Corinthians 5:21 NAS)

That is called the divine exchange. Jesus was made sin for us that we might be made righteous in Him with His righteousness. Satan's main weapon is taken from him. Jesus disarmed the principalities and powers by His death on Calvary's cross. He stripped them of their most powerful weapon against us, (to make us feel guilty). For the outworking of Christ's victory (see Colossians 2:15):

And having disarmed the powers and authorities [Satan's entire kingdom], He made a public spectacle of them, triumphing over them, by the cross (NIV). Brackets are mine.

A triumph is not actually the winning of a victory; it is the celebration and demonstration of a victory; that has already been won. Jesus through his death on the cross, demonstrated to the entire universe his victory over the entire satanic kingdom.

Please know, Jesus did not win that victory for Himself; He did it for us! It is God's purpose that the victory should be *worked out* and *demonstrated through us.* In 2 Corinthians 2:14 Paul said,

"But thanks be to God, who always leads us in His triumph in Christ, and manifests through us the sweetest aroma of the knowledge of Him in every place" (NAS).

God always causes us to share Christ's triumph over Satan's kingdom. That means there is no place when we cannot visibly *share* the triumph of Christ over Satan's kingdom.

In Matthew 28:18-20, we are told: Then Jesus came to them and said,

"All authority in heaven and on earth has been given to me. Therefore, go and make disciples of all nations, baptizing them in the name of the Father and of the Son and of the Holy Spirit, and teaching them to obey everything I have commanded you. And surely, I am with you always, to the very end of the ages." (NIV).

Here Jesus said that through His death on the cross, He has taken back the authority that Satan took from Adam, and He has vested it in all believers. "Therefore"? It's like Him saying, "I've taken Adam's authority back from Satan – and given it to you, now go and exercise it! You go and demonstrate My victory to the whole universe *by fulfilling My commission!*" *To God we give all the glory! Amen!*

STUDY GUIDE: WORKSHEET & REFLECTIONS CHAPTER 20

1. We are living in a day when many believe that biblical Christianity is _____, and not good enough for today's situations, so they retreat to science and _____.

2. Fasting and prayer help us to focus our power and full attention on the various _____ available in our Great Healer.

3. We are controlled not by our sinful nature, but by the _____ if the Spirit of God resides in us. (see Romans 8:9)

4. Our bodies are temples of the _____ _____ _____.

5. When God pulled us out of the world – He cut us away from what we were. He cut us away to be a new creation. (see 2 Cor. 5:17)

6. The writer of Hebrews admonishes us all to, "Pursue peace with all people, and holiness, without which no one will see the Lord .... ." (see Hebrews 12:14 NKJV)

7. All believers should be motivated to lay aside every weight, and sin which so easily ensnares us, and run with endurance the race that is set before us, looking unto Jesus, the author and finisher of our faith. (see Hebrews 12;1-2)

Chapter Twenty-One

PASS IT ON

*"For God so loved the world that He gave
His only begotten Son." (John 3:16)*

The Gospel truth of Jesus Christ is never more than *one generation* away from *extinction.* Many did not pass it on to their children in the bloodline. It must be guarded, protected and handed on for them to do the same, or *one day we will spend our autumn years* telling our children and our children's children what it was once like in the United States where people honored God, and Jesus Christ through the power of the Holy Spirit, and a Biblical Worldview.

The story is told of a young upstart asking his superiors why Coca Cola spent so much money on advertisement for such an internationally known product, as coca cola? The sympathetic executive told him, that each day millions die around the world who knew about coca cola; however, there are millions born each day who have never heard of coca cola. He continued coca cola is always one generation from extinction. It is imperative that we tell people the gospel truth of Jesus Christ every day!

Despite a growing hostile climate, true concerned followers of Christ are still magnifying the gospel of Jesus Christ – by His blood, by the word of their testimony, and an intimate relationship with Him.

It's crucial that we reclaim the truth that one role of the preacher and Bible teacher is to expose error and to reveal sin.

EVERY MEMBER A PRIEST (INTERCESSOR)

Today, many people are asking, "Where is Jesus Christ at work in the world today? How does He minister to the many problems of society today, as we move swiftly toward the end of the first quarter of the twenty-first century?" Surprisingly, to many, He is at work exactly as He was at work during His lifetime on earth, with the same strategy.

Notice, two thousand years ago, He did His work through one earthly *physical body*. Today, He carries on the same work through a complex, corporate body that exists worldwide, permeating and penetrating every level of society. It is "ecclesia," "the church," the body of Christ – but its ministry is to the same humanity that Jesus ministered to, with the same issues and conditions, along with the same attitudes and problems.

As stated earlier, our Lord has through the Holy Spirit empowered His corporate body with an assortment of spiritual gifts, designed to establish and improve relationship between any individual and God. The Holy Spirit is resident in the body (temple) of each believer.

Empowered and gifted by the Holy Spirit, we are the vessels or extension of Jesus's incarnate life through whom He continues His work on earth. It is only through their spiritual gifts in the power of the Holy Spirit that the spiritually fruitful individual (anointed and appointed) can function properly for Christ. Otherwise, his or her activity is only that of the "natural" man or yet "carnal" (in the "flesh").

REACHING THE WORLD FOR CHRIST

When considering the spiritual gifts and the Spirit in which they operate, we must never forget the two-fold purpose for the manifestation of these gifts. They are clearly given to work in *two* realms, the world and the church:

1. Unto the work of the ministry
2. Unto the building up of the body of Christ

We must be ever mindful that the work of the ministry *is to* the world. The church exists to be God's instrument to *reach* the world. "For God so loved the world that He gave His only Son." (John 3:16)

1. Clearly it is God's intention that the true church will move out into the world – so that the world might see Jesus Christ at work. The world needs His ministry so desperately today!
2. But He never intended that the world should have to come to the church to find Christ.
3. God designed the body of Christ to be incarnate in the world, present in the world, visible in the marketplaces and the public squares of the world.
4. If the people of the world are able to see the body of Christ among them, *ministering* to them, *challenging* them, *loving* them, *reaching* them, they will understand that Jesus Christ is very much alive today – *He is* here *among them*, in the person of ordinary believers.

ACCORDING TO PROMISE

According to His promise, Jesus has not left His people here to struggle and fidget around until the rapture. Christ is alive and working as He has done for more than two thousand years. Just as He said He would be: *"Behold I am with you always, to the close of the age."* (Matthew 28:20 ESV)

The question may be asked, what *specifically,* is the ministry of the body of Christ? Then, listen to Jesus's answer to that question.

In the synagogue He calls for the scroll of the prophet Isaiah, and – unrolling it to the proper place, Isaiah 64, and He reads:

*"The Spirit of the Lord is upon Me because He has anointed Me to **preach** the good news to the poor. He has sent Me to **proclaim release** of the captives and **recovering of sight** to the blind, to **set at liberty** those who are **oppressed,** to **proclaim** the acceptable year of the Lord.'* And He closed the book and gave it back to the attendant and sat down; and the eyes of all in the synagogue were fixed on Him. And He began to say to them. *Today this Scripture has been fulfilled in your hearing."* (Luke 4:18-21) Emphasis is mine throughout.

The Messiah would no doubt begin on that level in order to capture attention and evoke trust in Himself, but He would also fulfill a deeper and more important level – the level of the **(saved** human spirit):

Many of our people are dying of spiritual starvation because they don't know the Bible's whole story, and thus they do not find themselves in the story. Oh, it's true they may know many little stories and even hear 1 or 2 sermons a month, but is that adequate? Should Prayer Meeting/ Bible Study continue together? Or would they be more effective as two separate ministries of the church? A little bit of knowledge is not the big picture. Herein lies the value of expository preaching and teaching. As we preach and teach, we need to bring the passage of Scripture (text) into accountability with the big story of Scripture. When you preach and teach, help people to know the beginning, the middle, and the end – creation, fall, redemption, and consummation. By doing this,

1. You show your people who they are and where they are going.
2. You help them to incorporate their batch of little stories into God's grand metanarrative.
3. You will help them to press on with burning hearts toward maturity, and completeness in Christ.
4. We want the people to leave the preaching, teaching, witnessing event or conversation asking the right questions:

If our presentation is too small, their questions will be small. If we neglect the big story, the gospel metanarrative, they will be satisfied with small questions and will live on small insights. They may take home an insight, a story, or a principle.

However, we should not be satisfied with that, nor should they be satisfied. Our goal – our obsession should be nothing less than to exhort so that the congregation *sees* the big story of the gospel through every passage of Scripture. And let us pray that they might ask, to be given the power of the Word of God. "Did our hearts not burn within us, as the Scriptures were explained to us?"

Since postmodernists believe all truth is socially constructed, all presentations of absolute, universal, established truth *must* be resisted! Therefore, to them all grand and expansive accounts of truth, meaning, and existence, they cast aside as "metanarratives" that claim much more than they can deliver. The problem with this thinking is that Christianity without the gospel has no meaning.

If we don't counter this attack it will hurt our future efforts with generations Y and Z. Postmodernism was first developed in academia, but it has swiftly spread throughout the culture. This or any other new movement cannot be helpful to Christianity if their primary goal is to destroy Christianity.

I read an account about a young man who claimed to be a Christian and professed belief in Christ and love for the Bible – but he also *believed in reincarnation.*

His pastor confronted this belief in reincarnation by directing the young man to Hebrews 9:27. The text read, *"It is appointed for men to die once and after that comes judgment."* (NASB). The young man looked at his pastor and replied, **"Well that's your interpretation."** The young man simply *refused* to be instructed and bound by the biblical text.

In too many of our churches, the Bible is nearly silent.

A wild "thought" from academia [quickly spread throughout the culture], probably sponsored by the devil himself, who is no doubt laughing at those pastors, teachers, and churches, who are accepting that same answer concerning other sins such as fornication, same gender sexual relations, same sex marriages, cohabitation, sins like lying, unholy behaviors, and worldly lifestyles [all offering a *refusal to be instructed and bound by a biblical text*].

Sadly, the postmodern view is challenging the churches' biblical worldview for their own secular beliefs – through their "therapeutic theology" or throwing in "we are to welcome and love everybody." Many churches have chosen to "go along" in order to "get along."

THIS IS OUR STORY

Our story begins with *creation* by the omnipotent God, continues through the *fall of humanity into sin,* and the *redemption* of sinners, the *substitutionary work of Christ on the cross and, promises* finally an eternal destiny for all humanity – the redeemed with God forever in Glory – and the unredeemed in eternal punishment. This is the message we preach and teach, and it is a life-transforming and world-changing metanarrative. As the children of God, we must stand against:

- The claim that biblical truth is merely true for us.
- Our claim is that the Bible is the Word of God for all people.

We know this claim is deeply offensive to the postmodern worldview, which charges all who claim universal truth, with imperialism and oppression. As truth is *denied,* therapy remains, the question today has moved from "what is true?" to "what makes me feel good?" This cultural trend has been developing for decades but has reached ecstatic proportions in recent years. In a postmodern world, all issues eventually revolve around "the self."

Therefore, the highest self-esteem is all that remains as the goal of many educational and theological approaches, with *"sin"* as a category *rejected as oppressive and harmful to self-esteem:*

1. Therapeutic approaches are *dominant* in a postmodern culture made of individuals uncertain whether truth exists

or not – but are assured our self-esteem is healthy and in place.

2. Right and wrong are discarded as out-of-date reminders of an oppressive past.

3. The claim to divine revelation is written off as only one more projection of oppressive power that must be resisted.

4. The postmodern notion of the "death of the author" takes on an entirely new meaning when applied to Scripture, for we claim that the Bible is not the mere words of men but the *Word of God.*

5. Postmodernism's insistence on the death of the author is inherently anti-supernaturalistic and ultimately atheistic.

6. The young man in the earlier example was simply unwilling to be instructed and bound by the biblical text. Postmodernism claims that, anything can be explained away *as a matter of interpretation.*

7. In the name of our own "authenticity," we will reject all inconvenient moral standards and *replace* concern for right and wrong with the assertion of our rights.

8. Theology is likewise reduced to therapy. Entire theological systems and approaches are constructed with the goal reduced to nothing more than self-esteem for individuals and special groups.

9. The Bible is subjected to radical reinterpretation, with little or no thought for the simple meaning of the text or the clear intention of the human author.

10. Texts that are not pleasing to the *postmodern mind* are *rejected* as oppressive, patriarchal, heterosexist, homophobic, or deformed by some other political or ideological bias. The authority of the text is *denied in the name of liberation,* and the most fancy and *ridiculous interpretations* are celebrated as "affirming" and thus "authentic."

11. The rise of *feminist, liberation, homosexual,* and various other interest-group schools of interpretation is central to this *postmodern principle.* [64]

---

[64]   R. Albert Mohler, Jr. *He is not Silent* (Moody Publishers, Chicago, IL. 2008) 116-121

Because postmodern culture is committed to a *radical vision* of liberation, all authorities must be overthrown, including texts, authors, traditions, metanarratives, the Bible, God, and all powers in heaven and on earth. All authority is denounced, deconstructed, and thrown aside, except, for the authority of the postmodern theorists and cultural figures themselves, who weld their power in the name of oppressed peoples everywhere.

Christians – especially Christian preachers and teachers – are seen as representatives of this autocratic deity and are to be resisted as authorities as well. Doctrines, traditions, creeds, and confessions – all these are to be *rejected* and *charged* with limiting self-expression and representing oppressive authority.

Preachers, and teachers are tolerated so long as their therapeutic messages are of enhanced self-esteem; but are rejected whenever they inject divine authority or universal claims to *truth* in their sermon or teaching.

DISPLACEMENT OF MORALITY

Morality along with other foundations of culture, is discarded by postmodernists as *oppressive* and *totalitarian*.

A pervasive *moral relativism* marks postmodern culture!

However, the issues of moral concern, end up in many cases, a reversal of biblical morality. For example the issue of homosexuality, the rise of gay and lesbian studies in universities, gender reassignment, the emergence of homosexual political power, and the homoerotic images so common in the popular culture – a shocking reversal. Another shocking reversal is the fact that homosexuality is no longer considered *sin*, that is in postmodern culture; but "homophobia" is now *targeted* as the real sin and demands *tolerance of "alternative lifestyles."*

There are public *celebrations* of all lifestyles as morally equal. The very idea of perversity has become perverse to postmodern culture. Everything is permitted. So, those who participate in such activities as parades and the like today, boldly dress at home (banners and all).

OUR RESPONSE TO THE CHALLENGE

How should the body of Christ preach in the face of such confusion? Today the reality of *truth* itself is denied, as most persons think their most basic problems are rooted in a lack of self-esteem, *and when personal choice* is the <u>all-determining reality of the marketplace</u>:

1. How should we go about proclaiming and defending a gospel that declares to people that they are sinners in need of the one and only Savior, Jesus Christ?

    I would argue that this is a *critical time* of cultural and intellectual confusion – the task of preaching, and teaching must be understood as an apologetic calling.

2. *Apologetics – is the task of setting forth the* **truth claims of Christianity – and arguing for the unique truthfulness of the Christian faith.** I would argue that we must inform "the understanding" of every Christian, of his or her task of responsibility to truth of the gospel and true faith in a postmodern age.

In Acts 17:16-34, we see in Paul a good model for carrying out an apologetic argument in defense of truth in the passage above. While at the same time, he models the Great Commission proclamation. The scene on Mars Hill drew Paul's spiritual concern, not an intellectual "better than attitude" or scorn, as he observed the spiritual confusion of the Athenians. Today, it is a similar situation as we observe the spiritual confusion in the American culture. We should experience the same spiritual concern.

So, we preach Christ because we have met Him as our Savior, we were absorbed by the gospel, and we have been *transformed* by the *renewing of our minds*. Our preaching, teaching and Christian witness is not a matter of intellectual pride, but of spiritual concern! I wonder if we are grieved as we observe our American culture as Paul was in his observation of Athens.

We live in a nation of people who no longer want the true and living God, but *self*-realization, consumerism, comfort, pleasure, *psychological* salvation, sexual ecstasy, ambition, power, and success. By the millions, Americans embrace the new spiritualities (same old stuff with new labels) in an attempt for personal fulfillment and *self-transcendence*.

Once again, ancient paganism of nature worship has emerged along with multicultural religions and occult practices. As Journalist Walter Truett observes,

"Never before has any civilization made available to it populace such a smorgasbord of realities. Never before has a communications system like contemporary mass media made information about religion – all religions – available to so many people. Never has a society allowed its people to become consumers of beliefs – all beliefs – to become merchandise."[65] He says, America has become the "belief basket of the world."

I fear that we have adjusted to the "age" and Satan's "big lie." Acculturated, spiritually blind, and too shallow with the "isms" and idolatries all around us. We demand a comfort level that Paul and, the early church would deem scandalous! Where are the courageous men and women, who understands an *apologetic calling* at this critical time of (cultural and intellectual transition) in America and the world – the tasks of preaching, teaching, and practical Christian living must be *understood* as a calling! I repeat, Apologetics – the task of *setting forth* the *truth claims of Christianity* and *arguing for the unique truthfulness of the Christian faith*.

---

[65] Walter Truett Anderson, *Reality Isn't What It Used to Be* (San Francisco: Harper & Row, 1990), 188.

Authentic Christian preaching and teaching both *declares* and *defends* the *whole gospel* – *the center* of our proclamation is *Jesus Christ the Savior*, who was crucified for sinners, raised by the Power of God, (Holy Spirit), is coming again in glory and in judgment – and is now sitting and ruling at the right-hand of God the Father Almighty.

We must defend the:

- Truths of Christ's deity
- The truth of the virgin birth
- The truth of miracles
- The truth of the incarnation
- The reality of His substitutional death
- The assurance of His bodily resurrection
- The reality and ministry of the Holy Spirit

We can't just stop with these affirmations. We must place the person and work of Christ within the context of God's eternal purpose to reconcile people back to Himself – for His glory!

STUDY GUIDE: WORKSHEET AND REFLECTION
CHAPTER 21

1. Despite a growing hostile climate, _____ _____ followers of Christ continue to magnify the gospel of Jesus Christ – by His blood, by their word of testimony, and an intimate relationship with Him.

2. The twofold purpose for the manifestation of spiritual gifts – they are clearly given to work in two realms the _____ and the _____.

3. We must ever be mindful that the "work of the ministry" is to the _____.

4. The church exists to be God's _____ to reach the world. For God so loved the world that He gave His only Son" (John 3:16).

5. Clearly it is God's intention that the true church will move out into the world – so that they might see _____ _____ at work. The world needs His ministry so desperately today.

6. God designed the body of Christ to be incarnate in the _____, and visible in the marketplaces and public squares of the world.

7. If the people of the world are able to see the body of Christ among them, _____ to them, _____ challenging them, loving them, reaching them they will understand that Jesus Christ is very much alive and present today. He is here among them in the person of ordinary believers.

AFTERWORD

The faithful Christian (apologist) does not teach that which merely has been historically believed by the church and is now believed by faithful Christians. Rather, he or she teaches out of their own *personal confession of belief.* All true Christian preaching, teaching, and living, set before us is *experiential* – set by one who is possessed by a *deep* theological passion, *specific* theological convictions, and an *eagerness to see these convictions* shared by their people.

The faithful apologist should stand ready to *define, defend,* and *document* his or her own deep convictions drawn from careful study of God's Word and knowledge of the faithful teaching of the church; and this message is not for pastors only. Every blood-washed, born from above Christian has that same responsibility in our (practical) Christian life witness to and toward others.

Once again, our model for this kind of stamina is the apostle Paul. Throughout the New Testament, Paul's *personal testimony* is intertwined with his theology. Paul asserted,

"For the excellence of the knowledge of Christ Jesus my Lord, for whom I have suffered the loss of all things, and count them as rubbish, that I may gain Christ and be found in Him, not having my own righteousness, which is from the law, but that which is through faith in Christ, the righteousness which is from God by faith; that I may know Him and the power of His resurrection, and the fellowship of His sufferings, being conformed to His death, if by any means, I may attain to the resurrection from the dead." (Philippians 3:8-11 NKJV)

Paul taught clearly, defended his case, and made clear that he embraced these very doctrines as the substance of the life he lived and his faith. The experiential nature of his teaching does not mean that the authority for theology lies in personal experience. To be true, the authority must *always* remain the Word of God. However, that does not mean experiential character of the person's theological calling is not important.

The congregation must be able to observe the pastor, or teacher, basing their lives and ministry upon these truths, not just preaching, and teaching them. These same truths are applied for all true believers today. In his commitment to Timothy to not only pass the truths of Scripture on to the next generation, pass on the basis of those truths – the Word of God itself!

"And the things that you have heard from me among many witnesses, commit these to faithful men who will be able to teach others also." (2 Timothy 2:2 NKJV)

As we follow Paul's instructions, we too must make it clear that the authority of our teaching comes from the Holy Spirit and the Word of God (Bible). If we teach the truth but fail to teach the source of truth, we will not succeed in passing on our faith. Our affirmations and actions have to be founded on God's Word or they will be little more than wishful thinking. In the end every preacher and teacher stands under the same mandate that Paul handed down to Timothy.

Paul had been vigilant in His service to God. Please note that he did not make these comments until the end of his life, until he was about to die. He did not presume or rely on his past service. Instead he persevered, struggled, and served God until the end. (see 1 Corinthians 9:24-27)

"Finally, there is laid up for me the crown of righteousness, which the Lord, the judge, will give to me on that Day, and not to me only but also to all who have loved His appearing." (2 Timothy 4:8 NKJV).

The Psalmist says,

"We will not hide them from their children
but tell them to the coming generation
the glorious deeds of the LORD, and His might,
and the wonders that He has done
He established a testimony in Jacob
and appointed a law in Israel,
which He commanded our fathers
to teach to their children,
so that they should set their hope in God,
and not forget the works of God,
but keep His commandments;
and that they should not be like their fathers,
a stubborn and rebellious generation,
a generation whose heart was not steadfast,
whose spirit was not faithful to God."
Psalm 78:4-8 ESV

Printed in the United States
by Baker & Taylor Publisher Services